UNDERSTANDING
JACK KEROUAC

Understanding Contemporary American Literature
Matthew J. Bruccoli, Series Editor

Volumes on

Edward Albee • Nicholson Baker • John Barth • Donald Barthelme
The Beats • The Black Mountain Poets • Robert Bly
Raymond Carver • Chicano Literature
Contemporary American Drama
Contemporary American Horror Fiction
Contemporary American Literary Theory
Contemporary American Science Fiction • James Dickey
E. L. Doctorow • John Gardner • George Garrett • John Hawkes
Joseph Heller • Lillian Hellman • John Irving • Randall Jarrell
William Kennedy • Jack Kerouac • Ursula K. Le Guin
Denise Levertov • Bernard Malamud • Jill McCorkle
Carson McCullers • W. S. Merwin • Arthur Miller
Toni Morrison's Fiction • Vladimir Nabokov • Gloria Naylor
Joyce Carol Oates • Tim O'Brien • Flannery O'Connor
Cynthia Ozick • Walker Percy • Katherine Anne Porter
Reynolds Price • Thomas Pynchon • Theodore Roethke
Philip Roth • Hubert Selby, Jr. • Mary Lee Settle
Isaac Bashevis Singer • Jane Smiley • Gary Snyder
William Stafford • Anne Tyler • Kurt Vonnegut • James Welch
Eudora Welty • Tennessee Williams • August Wilson

UNDERSTANDING
JACK
KEROUAC

Matt Theado

University of South Carolina Press

© 2000 University of South Carolina

Published in Columbia, South Carolina, by the
University of South Carolina Press

Manufactured in the United States of America

04 03 02 01 00   5 4 3 2 1

Library of Congress Cataloging-in-Publication Data

Theado, Matt, 1959–
    Understanding Jack Kerouac / Matt Theado.
      p. cm. — (Understanding contemporary American literature)
    Includes bibliographical references (p.) and index.

    ISBN 1-57003-272-6
    1. Kerouac, Jack, 1922–1969—Criticism and interpretation.
  2. Beat generation in literature. I. Title. II. Series.
PS3521.E735 Z9 2000
813'.54—dc21   98-40291

For
my family and friends

CONTENTS

EDITOR'S PREFACE

The volumes of *Understanding Contemporary American Literature* have been planned as guides or companions for students as well as good nonacademic readers. The editor and publisher perceive a need for these volumes because much of the influential contemporary literature makes special demands. Uninitiated readers encounter difficulty in approaching works that depart from the traditional forms and techniques of prose and poetry. Literature relies on conventions, but the conventions keep evolving; new writers form their own conventions—which in time may become familiar. Put simply, *UCAL* provides instruction in how to read certain contemporary writers—identifying and explicating their material, themes, uses of language, points of view, structures, symbolism, and responses to experience.

The word *understanding* in the titles was deliberately chosen. Many willing readers lack an adequate understanding of how contemporary literature works; that is, what the author is attempting to express and the means by which it is conveyed. Although the criticism and analysis in the series have been aimed at a level of general accessibility, these introductory volumes are meant to be applied in conjunction with the works they cover. They do not provide a substitute for the works and authors they introduce, but rather prepare the reader for more profitable literary experiences.

M. J. B.

ACKNOWLEDGMENTS

I received much help and support in finishing this book. I would like to thank James T. Jones and Carolyn Cassady, who read the manuscript and offered valuable suggestions and insights. I also wish to express my appreciation for the support of my friends, especially Tim Cummings, Susan Gregory, and Jennifer Cheek.

CHRONOLOGY

Date of Composition	Date of Publication	Title
1946–48	1950	*The Town and the City*
1948–50		Various drafts of *On the Road*
1951	1957	*On the Road* (sometimes referred to as the "scroll version")
1951–52	1972	*Visions of Cody*
1952	1959	*Doctor Sax*
1953	1959/58	*Maggie Cassidy / The Subterraneans*
1955	1960/59	*Tristessa / Mexico City Blues*
1956	1963	*Visions of Gerard*, first half of *Desolation Angels*
1957	1958	*The Dharma Bums*
1961	1965/63	complete *Desolation Angels / Big Sur*
1965	1966	*Satori in Paris*
1967	1968	*Vanity of Duluoz*

UNDERSTANDING
JACK KEROUAC

INTRODUCTION

Jack Kerouac's published work presents an unwieldy accretion. His books include fiction, poetry, nonfiction, selected letters, religious writing, and the "true-story novels" for which he is most famous. At his death in 1969, twelve years after he became celebrated as the author of the best-selling *On the Road* (1957), he left at least eighteen published books and piles of unpublished writings, which are now appearing periodically in print. He devoted his life to writing, and his readers would have to devote themselves similarly to reading to pore through the literature that Kerouac amassed. Until recently, most people seemed to know of him more as a pop-culture icon that represents youth movements, quests of the spirit, and satiation of the senses with fast cars, jazz, drugs, and the pursuit of kicks. *Time* magazine's obituary refers to Kerouac's status as "shaman" of the Beat Generation who sounded his "barbaric yawp," yet the article never directly mentions that he was a writer. In the last fifteen years, especially since the first major Beat Generation conference at the Naropa Institute in 1982, scholars have been blasting the accumulated cultural debris from the excavation pit that had swallowed Kerouac's neglected—and often out-of-print—work. Still, with his resurgence in popularity, recently published work, and new academic momentum in support, Kerouac's work may seem paradoxically more ungainly than before. Now that he avoids the easy labels ("Beat Bard," "Daddy of the Hippies," "a literary James Dean") scholars, critics, and most of all new readers are continually reevaluating or discovering for the first time their takes on Kerouac.

Despite his goal to create a legend of his life in his writing, Jack Kerouac's work has never been satisfactorily fit into a unified scheme. He was the first to fail at the task. In the early 1950s Kerouac began to call his combined life's work the "Duluoz Legend." By February 1955 Kerouac wrote that he had "only ONE BOOK to write, in which everything, past, present, and future . . . is caught like dust in the sunlight" (*Some of the Dharma* 277). He explained that this one book is the Duluoz Legend, the ongoing story of his own life as he lived it, and he sought to share insights with his readers as he discovered them himself. In the introduction to *Big Sur,* written in 1961, Kerouac declared that all his work thus far comprised chapters in the Duluoz Legend and that in his later years he planned to provide uniform names for his characters and to assemble his various works into a cohesive whole. The Duluoz Legend, he claimed, "forms one enormous comedy, seen through the eyes of poor Ti Jean (me), otherwise known as Jack Duluo" (v). He died before completing or unifying his work as he had projected. Critics, too, point out Kerouac's failure to raise his life's adventures to legendary status in prose in a unified way.[1]

His first completed novel is *The Town and the City,* a fictionalized rendition of his own youth modeled on the romantic prose style of Thomas Wolfe and the human sympathy of William Saroyan. After that, Kerouac wrote much more directly from the events and significance of his own life in a style that was all his own. One may conveniently approach the form of the Duluoz Legend by arranging the novels according to their correlation to events in Kerouac's life without regard for the order in which he actually wrote the books. Ann Charters suggests such an order: "The Legend of Duluoz," she writes in *Kerouac,* his first biography,

> begins with *Visions of Gerard,* his earliest years, continues into his boyhood with *Doctor Sax* and adolescence with *Maggie Cassidy,* then goes on with *Vanity of Duluoz* into his college years and earliest encounters with [William] Burroughs and [Allen] Ginsberg. *On the Road* picks up when he met [Neal] Cassady, mid-way into the writing of *The Town and the City. Visions of Cody* describes the cross-country trips and conversations with Cassady after Jack had discovered spontaneous prose. *Lonesome Traveler* and *The Subterraneans* describe his years working, traveling, and living in New York, filled with the frustration of being unable to sell any manuscripts after his first book. *Tristessa* describes the month in Mexico City before *The Dharma Bums,* while *Desolation Angels* continues after Berkeley to his summer as fire-watcher and the publication over a year later of *On the Road. Big Sur* describes his alcoholic breakdown after the assault of fame and *Satori in Paris* concludes with loneliness of his final trip to Brittany.[2]

Charters also notes, though, that Kerouac hoped his true legendary status would be tied to his stylistic breakthroughs in writing, not merely to his adventurous life. Unfortunately, Kerouac's books were published in a haphazard order, a circumstance which confused readers. They were published neither in biographical order nor in the order of their composition, but in the order that suited publishers' business dictates and occasionally their whimsy.[3] In her 1983 scholarly treatment of Kerouac's work, Regina Weinreich attempted to reorder the Legend by focusing on "the literary repetition of the events of Kerouac's life in his attempt to elevate the legend of his life to the level of myth" and the "'progressive' solution" Kerouac used to solve the stylistic problems this task presented.[4] She groups the novels according to the circular design she sees within each core work as it reflects the overall circular design of the Legend itself. Warren French, author of *Jack Kerouac,* presents a simpler organization that relies not on "the order the books were written or published, but, as nearly possible, in the chronological order of the events in Kerouac's own life upon which they were based."[5] That is, he presents his critical study based on Charters's suggested order, in which the Legend comes close to intensified autobiography. In fact, editor Charters effectively uses the biographical order in the *Portable Jack Kerouac* (1995), the closest thing yet that readers have to a unified published Duluoz Legend. French dismisses works that he feels are not properly of the Legend, generally for stylistic reasons, and provides an excellent overview of the remaining books. One problem with French's approach, though, is that it masks Kerouac's stylistic development (although he does consider it, of course) in a way that a different order would illuminate. In *Understanding the Beats* Edward Halsey Foster recommends that Kerouac's works be read in the order of their composition, as "they reflect important changes in Kerouac's aesthetic and thinking."[6]

INTRODUCTION

The following chapters detail the ways that each work in the Duluoz Legend presents its own particular challenges to the writer. In each case Kerouac drew upon events from his life and built a work that coheres as much from its thematic unity as it does from its language. Specifically, Kerouac used linguistic innovations not only to tell the story but also to convey the appropriate atmosphere, the "felt sense," of the story. However, he accomplished more than simply coloring or setting the mood of a work. The structures of his sentences, the rhythms and the juxtaposition of images, and the innovative phrases re-create the writer's feeling for the subjects of each work. In so doing, he manages frequently to relate the "truth" of a story whether or not his episodes adhere to biographical fact. In *Doctor Sax* Kerouac's language embodies the mysteries of adolescence and maturation; he recreates a four-year-old's heightened perceptions in *Visions of Gerard;* and he traces the paranoia of a temporary mental breakdown in *Big Sur.* One way the very different books cohere into his Duluoz Legend, then, is through their focus on innovative language for of the conveyance of truth.

The real legend of Jack Kerouac is the saga of a writer at work. As recognition for Kerouac's artistic achievement increases, the Duluoz Legend outgrows the genre of autobiography and becomes an intimate chronicle of a writer's stylistic maturation. The most sensible approach to a critical study of his books is to consider them in the order of their composition, for this is a better guide to the story of a growing and, near the end of his life, a fading writer. This study traces Kerouac's stylistic development as a crafter of language within the texts themselves.

Kerouac's first published novel, *The Town and the City,* is ambitious and contains much fine writing, yet it is still an apprentice work. Contained within *The Town and the City,* however, are the basic themes that Kerouac would develop and explore in the Duluoz Legend. *On the Road,* written in 1951, more than a year after he finished the first novel, represents Kerouac's break with his prose guide, a moment when Northrop Frye might say that Kerouac overcame his anxiety of influence under Thomas Wolfe. *On the Road,* although written quickly in a bold, no-holds-barred rush of storytelling, is not yet an example of "spontaneous prose," the jazzy, exploratory method of composition that Kerouac sometimes referred to as "wild form" or "deep form." Spontaneous prose is Kerouac's foremost literary characteristic and may yet be his chief claim to literary longevity. He relied on this new technique in most of his subsequent work. Kerouac's best work begins with *Visions of Cody,* written in late 1951 and 1952. Kerouac's spontaneous prose surprised or upset readers and critics with its innovative style as much as *On the Road* surprised and upset readers with its social and sexual recklessness and descriptions of quasi-criminal activities. Kerouac wrote *Visions of Cody* about Neal Cassady, the young man who initially told Kerouac that he wanted to learn to write from him and went on to become his best friend, his inspiration, and a representative for Kerouac in what he saw as the vanishing glory years of America. After *Visions of Cody* Kerouac turned inwardly to his own past in a series of books that make up the core of the Duluoz Legend. Perhaps Kerouac needed Neal Cassady's inspiration as mentor and subject before he could turn to the topics that became his life's obsession, the telling of his own story in his own way. Kerouac's story as a writer who suffers from his own success wraps up in *Big Sur*. This novel, finished in 1961, completes a great cycle of going out (*On the Road*) and returning (in *Big Sur* he vows to stay home with his mother) that is matched by the stylistic developments that mark each book—or step—of the way. Linguistically, *The Town and the City* is Kerouac's first stammering statement of self-proclamation, and *On the Road* is his first successful speech before he discovers the full potential of language in spontaneous prose. Kerouac comes full circle in *Big Sur* as he despairs of the purpose of writing in the first place and regrets the use he has made of his life and his friends as subjects. He closes the book with a writer's epitaph: "There's no need to say another word." But Kerouac lived to write several more works that were in some ways less successful than his best work. In his last work, *Vanity of Duluoz,* he attempts to infuse his writing with a fresh, innovative style. He does not, however, achieve the linguistic virtuosity he had attained in his best prose.

James Jones chose the metaphor of a map for his study *A Map of* Mexico City Blues. Jones defines his role as explicator thus: "Rather than casting myself as a tour guide, I prefer to see myself as a cartographer." Jones removes himself, and thus the authority of his perspective as critic, by saying that his "point is to make sure readers know they can find their way around the poem without the actual physical presence of a tour guide."[8] This study also presents a handle for grasping Kerouac's works that may be useful for the general reader by noting the common themes that run through the Legend and the ways these themes mutate and reappear. This examination also outlines Kerouac's development as a writer from book to book and his awareness of his writing self, in hopes of conveying the essential Duluoz Legend. Kerouac wrote from the materials of his life—as any writer must—but his boon to world literature is the freedom of language that he invented and developed for exploring personal, spiritual, and generational stories.

CHAPTER ONE

Biography and Background

To understand Jack Kerouac, readers must know a few things about his life. More than that of most novelists, Kerouac's "fiction" is generally autobiographical. As did Thomas Wolfe, his early literary model, Kerouac sought to make his life into art, and language was the medium of metamorphosis. He wrote directly from the experiences of his life, transforming the details into art via intensified language. Kerouac's chief influences include his immigrant, working-class roots; the death of his brother, Gerard, at an early age; his strong urge to be a great writer; the death of his father and the subsequent close ties to his mother; the Beat Generation; his explorations of Buddhism and Catholic mysticism; and alcoholism. He pictured his entire life's work as "one enormous comedy" which he called the Duluoz Legend.

Jean Louis (Jack) Kerouac was born March 12, 1922, in Lowell, Massachusetts, a mill town on the Merrimack River. The last of three children, Kerouac had an older brother, Gerard, and older sister, Caroline. In *Doctor Sax* (1959) Kerouac claims to remember the day (17). As Kerouac grew, he amazed his friends with his prodigious feats of memory and earned the nickname "Memory Babe." Whether or not he actually recalled the day of his birth, his memory served him throughout his career as a writer. Nearly all of Kerouac's books consist of events recalled from his past. For example, *Visions of Gerard* (1963) covers the first years of Kerouac's life and focuses on the death of his older brother, Gerard, of rheumatic fever when Kerouac was four years old. Kerouac continued the chronology of the legend with *Doctor Sax,* a book that covers his adolescent years.

Kerouac's parents, Leo and Gabrielle, were of French-Canadian heritage, and Kerouac grew up speaking French rather than English; he remained bilingual throughout his life. Some questions persist over whether Kerouac's family spoke French or a Franco-American hybrid called *joual* which biographer Tom Clark claims is spoken by the Quebecois.[1] Readers interested in Kerouac's use of French may wish to consult *Visions of Cody* (1972, 362–63) to see parallel passages he wrote in French and English. The effect of his childhood language is difficult to gauge, but maybe Kerouac's inventiveness in the English language was born from his need to discover meanings on the fly, so to speak. In Lowell he grew up among the tenements and back alleys of blue-collar families with Irish, Greek, and French-Canadian backgrounds, and he heard not only various languages but also unique inflections and dialects. Kerouac once distinguished a basic difference between himself and Denver native Neal Cassady: "You never spoke my tongue nor lived in foreign neighborhoods . . . it was I, sad grownup Jack of today, mooning ragtail among the tincans and clinkers, in the hot strange sun and jabbering hum of French-Canadian time" (*Letters* 255). Kerouac later wrote that when he enrolled at school, he did not yet speak English fluently and that as late as age eighteen he spoke English haltingly (*Doctor Sax* 3). His childhood French language appears in several of his books, most notably in *Doctor Sax* and *Visions of Gerard.* French was apparently often the language of his thoughts; he once told friend and poet Allen Ginsberg that he was writing from the French in his head (*Letters* 383), and he also wrote a short novel in French (*Letters* 395). His early lack of confidence with English hindered neither his desire nor his ability to write. In fact, he once attributed his skill in writing to the acquisition of English. He claimed that his facility in using English rose from the very fact that it was not his first language; he modified English to suit the "French images" in his head (*Letters* 229). As he matured, his voice became an amalgam of his experiences in travel and even in reading. In *Desolation Angels* (1965) Kerouac writes that his voice—and he refers to his *writing* voice as well—is a blend of "French-Canadian and New York and Boston and Okie accents all mixed up and even Espanol and even Finnegans Wake" (87).

As a child Kerouac drew comics for his friends. He wrote an adolescent novel, a collection of short stories, a second novel at age twenty-one, and a collaborative effort with William Burroughs, who later would write *Naked Lunch,* all before his first formally conceived and fully developed novel, *The Town and the City* (1950). In addition, Kerouac was an insatiable letter writer, and he briefly wrote sports coverage for his hometown newspaper, a jazz column for his prep school, and various short stories and poems. He once told William Burroughs that he had written a million words by the time he was eighteen years old.

Kerouac credited Gerard's inspiration in his writing. As attested to in his letters and in *Visions of Gerard,* Kerouac knew his brother to be a saint, a pure young boy who saw angels and had visions of heaven. He rescued trapped mice and spoke to birds on the windowsill, acts Kerouac would later imitate. Kerouac saw his brother as a holy figure more concerned with eternity than with the mundane life. In *Visions of Gerard* Kerouac describes a morning when the schoolchildren were lining up. Young Gerard strays from the class while musing on the nature of God, and he is scolded by a nun: "Gerard Duluoz, you're not in line—!" (28). In this passage Gerard is both nonconformist and self-involved, traits that characterize Kerouac's writing as well. First publishers and then critics would tell Kerouac that his new prose and mystical themes were "not in line" with their expectations.

Gerard's death after a two-year illness left a vacancy in the Kerouac household and a continuing guilt for the remaining brother, who pondered that it should have been him, the less worthy one, to have died. Kerouac developed an obsession with suffering and death that would eventually lead him to Buddhism for answers to mankind's pain. Gerard first imparted to Kerouac the Buddhist awareness he would come to later in his life: "All is Well, practice Kindness, Heaven is Nigh" (*Visions of Gerard* 6).

Kerouac was a standout athlete, excelling at baseball, football, and track. Biographer Gerald Nicosia reports that in high school Kerouac was a football hero who scored the winning touchdown in the big Thanksgiving Day game in front of fourteen thousand spectators.[2] Yet Kerouac was more than a jock at Lowell High School; he was an excellent student as well. His future seemed bright, for he was at once athletic and intelligent, popular with other students, and admired by girls. Two teenage friendships are especially important. The first was with Mary Carney, a young woman of Irish descent. Kerouac and Carney became romantically involved, and even though they were together for a relatively short time, she always represented for Kerouac the simple, small-town life he might have had if he had settled down in Lowell and become a mill worker. In a sense, Kerouac spent his youth living the Great American Dream among other immigrant families who labored and learned and loved. They went to church and to school; they played out epic baseball and football games on the sandlots; they ate big suppers and read *The Shadow* magazine and listened to the radio at night. Kerouac's father was a printer by trade, an appropriate occupation for a young writer to know. Yet as Kerouac reached young manhood, he felt the split between his small-town roots and the possibilities that lay ahead in the city: university, football fame, a bohemian writer's life, adventure. One of the important themes of *The Town and the City,* as suggested by its title, is the great cultural break between the neighborly, family-centered life in Lowell and the rather immoral, decadent life in the city. Kerouac dramatized his relationship with Mary Carney in *The Town and the City,* and he dealt with it explicitly in a later book, *Maggie Cassidy* (1959): "From sweet Lowell Maggie came to sour New York in a rosy gown. . . . A little rose in her hair—the perfection of her moonlight magic Irish sorcery—suddenly seeming out of place in Manhattan" (178–79). Finally Maggie decides that Jack must choose between her and New York (182). James Jones indicates Kerouac's use of Oswald Spengler's *The Decline of the West* in his awareness of the development from culture to civilization, manifested by the rise of the city over the town (9). Biographer Charles Jarvis, one of Kerouac's acquaintances from Lowell, suggests that Maggie Cassidy "might have been the idealized woman that men live with in the realm of their beautiful dreams. . . . Maggie Cassidy is everybody's first love."[3]

Another youthful friendship represented a possible middle path between the town and the city, between the desire for artistic success and a hometown connection. Sebastian "Sammy" Sampas was a Greek friend from Lowell who shared with Kerouac a passion for literature. While Kerouac frequently masked his literary aspirations out of shyness, Sampas boldly announced his desire to be a poet. Moreover, Kerouac projected the image of a tough footballer, and he was often surprised to see Sammy burst into tears over mankind's plight, or into song and poetry with the slightest provocation. Kerouac shared with Sampas his enthusiasm for Thomas Wolfe while Sampas encouraged Jack to read the works of William Saroyan. Other of Kerouac's high school friends would wind up working in the Lowell mills, which Kerouac insisted he would avoid, while Sampas showed Kerouac that the life of an artist could be an end in itself. Together they searched for methods of artistic expression and dubbed themselves "Prometheans," although they battled over the exact meaning and approach to art that the term implied. Kerouac wrote in *Visions of Gerard* that he had seen "in the eyes of Gerard the very diamond kindness and patient humility of the Brotherhood Ideal" (7). He became aware of the same humility in Sampas. When he was twenty-one, Kerouac wrote to a girlfriend of his concerns for "humanism" and his association with like-minded friends, an early colloquy that broke ground for the Beat Generation: "We are obscure, and may never dent progress—but we have heated discussions and plenty of intellectual stimulation" (*Letters* 25). Sammy Sampas died in March 1944 after being wounded in Anzio. Kerouac lost utterly one of the Lowell connections with whom he mutually had struggled to understand art and the artist's life. His separation from Lowell's essence, though never complete in his life, was carried one step further along.

Kerouac's football skills were his ticket to New York City, where he spent a year at Horace Mann Preparatory School before enrolling at Columbia on a football scholarship. Although he showed promise as a halfback, he broke his leg early in his first year and did not play the rest of the season. He still dreamed of becoming a literary hero. He read widely—especially Thomas Wolfe—met new friends, and roamed "the vast and rich web of the city almost nightly" (*Letters* 10) in the leisure time now afforded him by his injury. Kerouac spent the World War II years alternately playing football and shipping out with the Merchant Marine. He was briefly in the navy, but he was discharged for psychiatric reasons. After returning to New York City in the spring of 1944, Kerouac centered himself near the Columbia campus and met the people who would change his life. Kerouac recounted his experiences on the football field, in the war, and afterward in New York in *Vanity of Duluoz* (1968).

Among the new friends Kerouac met was seventeen-year-old Allen Ginsberg, a first-year student from New Jersey. Like Sampas, Ginsberg was not shy about his literary aspirations. To all appearances, Kerouac, the football player-turned-seaman, and Ginsberg, a sensitive Jewish intellectual, were an unlikely pairing. In the next decade and beyond, they would push each other and compel each other to bring new artistry to their writing. Primarily, Ginsberg was a poet and Kerouac a prose writer, so there was no inherent rivalry in the production of their respective forms. Not long after they met, Kerouac wrote to Ginsberg of their mutual perceptions as artists: "I find in you a kindred absorption with identity, dramatic meaning, classic unity, and immortality: you pace a stage, yet sit in the boxes and watch. You seek identity in the midst of indistinguishable chaos, in sprawling nameless reality" (*Letters* 81). Ginsberg later recalled his initial meeting with Kerouac: "I remember being awed by him and amazed by him, because I'd never met a big jock who was sensitive and intelligent about poetry."[4] As different as the two men were, they were likeminded when it came to their idea that rather than being assured of a strong American future, they feared instead that America was on the brink of a decline. Kerouac and Ginsberg found in each other an opportunity to speak honestly, from their minds, rather than feeling the pressure of having to make trite or cliched exchanges. Kerouac was one of the first men Ginsberg told of his homosexuality. In Ginsberg, Kerouac found a companion who shared his love for a romanticized America and a desire to achieve greatness in writing. Ginsberg filled a role that previously might have been satisfied by Gerard and by Sammy Sampas; he was another brother, a fellow sufferer and visionary, one in whom the normally shy Kerouac could confide.

BIOGRAPHY AND BACKGROUND

Only a few months before meeting Ginsberg, Kerouac had met William Burroughs, who had come to him through a mutual friend to ask questions about shipping out in the merchant marine. Burroughs, of the Burroughs Adding Machine family, had been born to a privileged life in Saint Louis. His keen intelligence got him into Harvard in 1932, where he experimented with weapons and read about drugs. After graduation his parents provided him with a monthly stipend. He took the grand tour of Europe, then returned to America where he continued his education by taking courses in psychoanalysis and began to move among hustlers and petty criminals. Burroughs was brilliant and widely read, although he was not interested in a writing career at that time.

When Kerouac, Ginsberg, and Burroughs met, the core of the Beat Generation writers was set. For some time, Kerouac had been engaged in lengthy discussions with Ginsberg and fellow Columbia student Lucien Carr about the "New Vision," based in part on the ideals of their hero, French poet Arthur Rimbaud. Kerouac pinned a Rimbaud quotation on his wall: "When shall we go, over there by the shores and mountains, to salute the birth of new work, the new wisdom, the flight of tyrants, and of demons, the end of superstition, to adore . . . the first ones!" Lucien Carr had been responsible for introducing Kerouac to Burroughs and Ginsberg, and he was a key influence in their discussions. Inspired by the Russian novelist Fyodor Dostoevsky, these young men were attracted to the underground scene, lured by criminality. Kerouac now was hanging out with "the most evil and intelligent buncha bastards and shits in America" (*Vanity of Duluoz* 201). On August 14,

1944, Carr stabbed friend David Kammerer to death, an incident the New York tabloids sensationalized. Kerouac was detained as a material witness. Since Kerouac's father refused to help him make bail, he accepted girlfriend Edie Parker's offer: her family would loan him the one-hundred-dollar bail if he married her. On August 22 Kerouac was let out of jail long enough to get married, with a plainclothes detective acting as best man.

Kerouac's father did not approve of Jack's new friends. Shortly after Jack began writing *The Town and the City* in 1946, the book he hoped would prove to his father that he was a serious writer, his father died from cancer of the stomach. Jack was alone with him at the end, and Leo implored Jack to take care of his mother, a directive Kerouac never forgot. Kerouac worked steadily on the novel for the next two years, and by the spring of 1948 he had written 380,000 words. Ann Charters notes that Kerouac "had taken Thomas Wolfe as his model, but this book was really written for his father, to prove to the memory of Leo Kerouac that Jack could write a book that would sell, that he could make money as a creative writer" (65). While Kerouac was writing this book in the winter of 1946–1947, Neal Cassady entered his life. Hal Chase, another Columbia student, had known Cassady as a boyhood friend in Denver, and he had written him of his new philosophy-minded friends in New York. Although Kerouac was not immediately impressed with Neal, he soon came to see him as a new kind of American hero, one who would show him new ways of written expression and who would serve as the hero of some of Kerouac's best books.

According to legend, Cassady had stolen five hundred cars and been to bed with five hundred women by the time he was eighteen. The son of an alcoholic, he had been in and out of reform school several times. Although he had little formal education, he had a keen natural intelligence and an energetic curiosity. More important to Kerouac, though, was his addictive enthusiasm for life. Cassady was able to throw himself into adventures without regard for his own security; he moved with the moment. His tremendous energy and ability to engage in all-night talkfests as well as his ambivalent sexuality made him a natural complement to the New York gang. However, as Kerouac wrote in *On the Road* (1957), his other friends were either intellectuals or criminals who were bent on criticizing American culture; Neal was intelligent "without the tedious intellectualness," and his "'criminality' was not something that sulked and sneered; it was a wild yea-saying overburst of American joy" (10). In addition, Cassady reminded Kerouac of "some long-lost brother," a reference to Kerouac's lost heroes of his past, Gerard and Sammy. Cassady inspired Kerouac's on-the-road travels for which he would become legendary.

Initially Cassady had asked Kerouac to teach him to write. Four years later, in the winter of 1950, Kerouac received a long letter from Cassady that he recognized as a masterpiece worthy of Dostoevsky (*Letters* 242). Kerouac was especially impressed that Cassady held nothing back in the letter, that he incorporated the "painfully necessary" details of his thoughts as well as of specific locations, measurements, and chronology (243). Kerouac saw the importance of reliance on direct experience, and he was suddenly changed as a writer. He would no longer fictionalize his experiences into novels like the Wolfe-inspired *The Town and the City*. Instead, he would write from his life directly, infusing the scenes with his own artistic vision, tempered by Burroughs's matter-of-fact Dashiell Hammett approach to narrative. Thus Cassady is both hero and a stylistic influence for *On the Road*. Kerouac recalled eighteen years later that Cassady inspired the energetic style of *On the Road* via the letters he wrote to Kerouc: "all first person, mad, confessional, completely serious, all detailed. . . . I got the flash from his style" (Berrigan 541–42). In the spring of 1951 Kerouac furiously typed onto a 120-foot scroll of art paper fed through his typewriter a fast-paced, straightforward exploration that became *On the Road*. Cassady reappears as a character in *The Subterraneans* (1958), *The Dharma Bums* (1958), *Desolation Angels, Big Sur* (1962), and *Book of Dreams* (1961). Yet Kerouac's masterpiece, *Visions of Cody,* is the only book that focuses totally on Cassady as its sole subject. No other person affected Kerouac's artistic production as significantly as Cassady did.

The Town and the City was published in 1950 and received decent, though not outstanding, reviews. The book sold poorly. Kerouac had failed as a football star, and now he feared he was unsuccessful as a professional writer. Between 1950 and 1957 Kerouac wrote at least a dozen more books of both prose and poetry, yet none of the books was published (see chronology for list of books by date written and date published). During the seven years between the publication of *The Town and the City* and *On the Road,* Kerouac lived the adventures and wrote most of the books for which he is now famous. He moved among the bohemian circles in New York and in San Francisco; he listened to the bop musicians in jazz clubs; he lived on a rooftop in Mexico City; he climbed a California mountain with poet Gary Snyder; he spent a solitary summer as a mountain-top fire lookout in Washington; and all the while he traveled on freight trains or buses, hitchhiked, or rode shotgun while Neal Cassady sped through the American night, unspooling his continuous rap.

When Kerouac came off the road or returned from wild parties in Manhattan, he came home to his mother, Gabrielle, whom he began to call Memere. Kerouac was a split person, drinking in increasing amounts, smoking marijuana and taking Benzedrine and trying morphine with his friends, then returning to his mother who would cook him meals and look after his clothes. Kerouac and his mother shared a complex relationship, one that Kerouac critic James Jones suggests borders on the Oedipal. For the rest of his life, Kerouac was never far from his mother, and he wrote about his adult life with her in *Desolation Angels* (334). Kerouac's onetime lover and lifelong friend, Carolyn Cassady, agrees that "much of his attachment sprang from his Catholic conditioning, from his father's admonition, and from the fact that she loved him so much and took care of his physical needs." Yet Cassady does not find Kerouac's attachment to his mother excessive. Instead, she feels that, since Kerouac was so painfully shy with both strangers and acquaintances, "with her was the only time he could 'let it all hang out,' be completely himself, do and say anything, knowing she would love him and approve of him no matter what he did or said."[5] Since Kerouac also drew on his childhood experiences, some critics see a division between his "Lowell books" and his "Beat Generation books." Religion and spiritual topics constitute a third category as well—*The Scripture of the Golden Eternity* (1960) and *Some of the Dharma* (1997). Kerouac never stopped writing, and not even years of publishers' rejections could make him lose confidence in his genius. By the middle 1950s Kerouac was convinced that he had found his life's work. He was writing the story of his life, the Duluoz Legend. He wrote to Viking Press adviser Malcolm Cowley in September 1955 that there were seven books already completed in his Duluoz Legend, and he foresaw "millions" of words more before he would complete the Legend. Kerouac told Cowley that the spontaneous nature of his production resulted in rhythmic prose, an effect that greatly pleased the author (*Letters* 515).The Duluoz Legend is more than rhythm. Weinreich perceives that "since Kerouac is concerned with origins, as are all legend-makers, he depicts the fall of society in a grand design—American as well as Christian—that looks to recapture an original paradise or origin from which all else is a decline" (11).

In September of 1957 Viking Press finally published *On the Road,* and Kerouac, by now an underground legend in New York's Greenwich Village and San Francisco's North Beach, became an overnight nationwide celebrity. Ironically, his success initiated his failure. Kerouac was not suited for mass media fame. An extroverted "madman" in his writing, he was actually shy in public and often became ill at the thought of appearing on a television show or even at a book-signing party. His already heavy drinking increased.

References to "The Beat Generation" had been circulating in the press and popular media since John Clellon Holmes's *Go,* a roman à clef that concerns the lives and activities of Kerouac, Cassady, Ginsberg, and others, published in 1952. Interest in the Beat Generation led to Holmes's feature article in the *New York Times Magazine,* "This Is the Beat Generation," in which Holmes credits Kerouac with inventing the phrase. According to Holmes, being beat "implies the feeling of having been used, of being raw. It involves a sort of nakedness of mind, and, ultimately, of soul; a feeling a being reduced to the bedrock of consciousness."[6] Ginsberg's temporarily banned poem, "Howl," added in 1956 to the sensational attention foisted on the Beats. When Kerouac's *On the Road* hit the bestseller lists in 1957, though, the Beat Generation became a hot topic.

Gilbert Millstein, the *New York Times* writer who had solicited Holmes's Beat Generation article, reviewed Kerouac's book. Millstein predicted that *On the Road* would be for the Beat Generation what *The Sun Also Rises* was for the Lost Generation. Half of his review concerns the Beat Generation and its characteristics. Although Kerouac's book concerns the lives and times of those who made up the Beat Generation, the book is really about the pursuit of the American Dream in post–World War II society by several individuals seeking to be unfettered by conformism, materialism, and general social paranoia. As a new world power in the cold war era, some observers felt that America had come to exert a restraining force on the individual freedom of its own citizens. Kerouac had once promoted his book to publishers as a Beat Generation document, and he even once titled it "The Beat Generation." Nonetheless, readers would have to look carefully to find references to the Beat Generation in the text itself. If Viking—and

later paperback publishers Signet and Penguin—had not fea-
tured the Beat Generation in advertisements and book-cover
notes, it is likely that this book would not be so closely aligned
with the Beatnik craze that followed. Such alignment came at
the cost of Kerouac's own reputation as a "serious" writer. One
of the ironies of his life is that as a youth he had fantasized
about enjoying the literary success of a traditional author.
When success came, though, notoriety, not lionization, was his
fate.

Kerouac had identified a powerful social force in the late
1940s and labeled it with a catchy phrase. He also found universal spiritual connotations in the term *beat,* especially as it
implied the beatitudes and Kerouac's strong sense of
humankind's essential unity. In the summer of 1954 he
announced that he was "a member of the BEATIFIC GENER-
ATION" (*Some of the Dharma* 95), and he wrote to Allen Ginsberg at the same time that he saw "beatitude" in "beat," a word
he felt would be understood in all the Romance languages (*Letters* 434). In coming years, however, the phrase spun out of his
control. According to William Burroughs, "After 1957 *On the
Road* sold a trillion levis and a million espresso coffee
machines, and also sent countless kids on the road. This was of
course due in part to the media, the arch-opportunists. They
know a story when they see one, and the Beat movement was a
story, a big one."[7] After San Francisco newspaper columnist
Herb Caen dubbed the new writers "beatniks," a pejorative,
Yiddish-ized term, the Beat Generation became the Beatnik
Fad. Kerouac spent the rest of his life trying to explain his original intentions. Shortly after the publication of *On the Road* he

BIOGRAPHY AND BACKGROUND

asked a *New York Herald Tribune* interviewer, "Do you know what a beatnik is? . . . They write a line of poetry, type it up in a great big expensive five dollar binding book, put it under their arm, put on sandals, grow a little goatee, walk down the street and say they're poets. It's just kind of a fad. It was invented by the press. Listen, I'm a railroad brakeman, merchant marine deckhand in war time. Beatniks don't do those things. They don't want to work. They don't want to get jobs."[8] Kerouac's description of beatniks could have passed for the general impression the public was developing of Kerouac himself. A year and a half later Kerouac told Al Aronowitz of the *New York Post* that the Beat Generation "is not important, it's a fad. You see, this is silly, it has nothing to do with the serious artists who started the whole thing."[9] In 1967 Kerouac told an interviewer, "Oh, the beat generation was just a phrase I used in the 1951 written manuscript of *On the Road* to describe guys like Moriarty who run around the country in cars looking for odd jobs, girlfriends, kicks. It was thereafter picked up by the West Coast leftist groups and turned into . . . all that nonsense."[10] A year before his death, Kerouac explained on William Buckley's *Firing Line* television program that "in the papers they called it 'beat mutiny' and 'beat insurrection,' words I never used. Being a Catholic, I believe in order, tenderness, and piety."[11]

One cannot analyze Kerouac's lifework without simultaneously considering his life, as the two are deeply intertwined. Kerouac lived to write, and he looked into his own life for what he considered the most indispensable material. Essentially, writing justified his life. And his life—for readers—justifies his writing in that it helps explain its stylistic eccentricities.

Kerouac concludes *The Subterraneans,* a story of a doomed love affair, this way: "And I go home having lost her love. And write this book" (111). Even if he failed in love, he succeeded in art. Some observers may conclude that Kerouac failed in life—he never maintained a solid home life that he yearned for; he had a child he rarely saw; he was frequently broke and often depended on his mother; he died an early alcoholic's death— yet his work stands as a testament to his genius.

CHAPTER TWO

Kerouac's Technique

Strangely enough these scribblings were the first of their kind in the world, I was originating (without knowing it, you say?) a new way of writing about life, no fiction, no craft, no revising afterthoughts, the heartbreaking discipline of the veritable fire ordeal where you can't go back but have made the vow of "speak now or forever hold your tongue" and all of it innocent go-ahead confession.

—*Desolation Angels*

On the Road is the most talked about novel Kerouac wrote and for a long time was the most readily available. The novel is an adventure story set in the late 1940s about two men who travel in fast cars from coast to coast "in pursuit of kicks"—usually jazz, marijuana, and women. Although the book contains some energetic and evocative "widescreen travel writing" and jazzy descriptions of nightclub life, it is not a difficult read. Sal Paradise's adventures are contained in a linear narrative, and the tale itself is framed by Sal's "miserable weary split up" (3) from his first wife and marriage to his second, the woman he "had always searched for and for so long" (306). From this book the reader may go to *The Dharma Bums*, Kerouac's second most popular book. Viking originally published this novel a year after *On the Road* and packaged it as a sequel to the earlier book: "the two young men remain faithful in their fashion to their quest as Truth bums, and when we finally take leave of

them, each has caught sight of his goal and is on the road to it"
(dust-jacket notes on first edition). As in *On the Road,* Kerouac
wraps lyrical passages of writing in narrative prose that is otherwise well controlled. The reader may seek to read more
books, especially since twenty-odd Kerouac titles are currently
in print. *Tristessa* (1960) begins with these words:

> I'm riding along with Tristessa in the cab, drunk, with big
> bottle of Juarez Bourbon whiskey in the till-bag railroad
> lootbag they'd accused me of holding in railroad 1952—
> here I am in Mexico City, rainy Saturday night, myster-
> ies, old dream sidestreets with no names reeling in, the
> little street where I'd walked through crowds of gloomy
> Hobo Indians wrapped in tragic shawls enough to make
> you cry and you thought you saw knives flashing beneath
> the folds—lugubrious dreams as tragic as the one of Old
> Railroad Night where my father sits big of thighs in
> smoking car of night, outside's a brakeman with red light
> and white light, lumbering in the sad vast mist tracks of
> life— (7–8)

This present-tense, in medias res beginning offers few
footholds for the uninitiated reader. After the traditional opening of *On the Road* this book starts off disconcertingly. Kerouac introduces images with blurring speed, juxtaposing scenes
with dream and memory, mixing the real and the imagined, in
unorthodox sentences and phrases. The reader cannot simply
sit back and enjoy the ride, as in the other two books, for in this
text so far nothing is made clear. The reader must participate in

KEROUAC'S TECHNIQUE

the construction of meaning and enter Kerouac's world, "the one story that I always write about" (*Book of Dreams* 3).

The first few words are obvious enough; the narrator is in a cab with a woman named Tristessa, and he is drunk. The present-tense verbs suggest also that he (the first-person narrator) is drunk *now,* as the moments of the cab ride and of the composition merge in one present moment shared by the reader. The narrator's "overflow of feelings" is not recollected in Wordsworth's "moments of tranquility." No evidence suggests that Kerouac wrote this passage drunk, but his technique in recapturing the experience suggests intoxication with language and with the immediacy of the event. Kerouac often combines the past of the event and the present moment of the writing in his work. For example, early in the narration of *The Subterraneans* he describes his meeting with a girl and then adds that as he is typing he is listening to jazz singer Sarah Vaughan on the radio (2). To tie the event and the writing-about-the-event together Kerouac draws attention to the language and loads the first paragraph of *Tristessa* with jumbled neo-Kerouacisms, including "outside's a brakeman" and the compressed "till-bag railroad lootbag," a pure Kerouac sound echoed rhythmically in "sad vast mist tracks." Combined with dream images of his father and "old dream sidestreets," this first paragraph has a compression and a latent poetic power and is not simply the accretion of jumbled images it first appears to be.

Kerouac's contractions and verb use convey informality, more a heard voice than a polished read, all in a blur of motion ("I'm riding"). In his books Kerouac usually presents himself as a passenger, an observer, not the driver and agent of the

action. In *On the Road* Paradise shambles after those who interest him, and he is nearly always the passenger in a bus, in a
hitched ride, or in the right-hand seat at the mercy of Dean
Moriarty's mad driving. In *The Dharma Bums* Kerouac's alter
ego Ray Smith follows behind the mountain-climbing enthusiasm of Japhy Ryder.

One of the pleasures of reading Kerouac's Duluoz Legend
comes from discovering layers of details that overlap and connect one book with another. Kerouac was aware that this fusion
can present problems, since "readers who haven't read up to
this point in the earlier works are not filled in on the background" (*Desolation Angels* 229). In this case Kerouac wrote
about the "lootbag" in "October in the Railroad Earth" when he
described a "bag so bad a brakeman seeing me with it in the
San Jose yard coffee shop said whooping loud 'A railroad lootbag if I ever saw one!'" (70). In *Vanity of Duluoz* Kerouac
reveals why he bought the bag in the first place, for in "June
1942, with a little black bag containing rags and a collection of
classical literature" he boarded his ship (119). When the time
comes to begin his famous adventures on the road, he recounts
that he packed his canvas bag and departed for the west (*On the
Road* 12); he packs the same bag several years later on another
trip west (*Visions of Cody* 107).

A sense of impending remorse is prevalent in much of Kerouac's writing; for one thing, he relates that he feels guilty for
not staying longer with his railroad job (*Book of Dreams* 15).
Kerouac frequently mentions in his writing that he worked on
the railroad as a brakeman, a part of his life he explored thoroughly in "October in the Railroad Earth." He uses this and his

employment in other working-class jobs to dissociate himself from the more affluent and elegant writers who earn their livings through writing and to emphasize his equality with his coterie of lower-class heroes such as Dean Moriarty and Tristessa—and of the Beat Generation.

Kerouac involves *Tristessa* in his "one story" that he always writes about by repeating key images in his other books throughout his career. Here Kerouac reintroduces one of his favorite images, the rainy night. *The Town and the City* is filled with rain; Sal Paradise tells a girlfriend of his Myth of the Rainy Night in *On the Road;* and an early title for *Doctor Sax* was "The Myth of the Rainy Night." In *The Subterraneans* Kerouac clarifies the importance of rain as a unifying device that suggests the power of his own literature, for the rain "kiss[es] everywhere men and women and cities in one wash of sad poetry" (25).

Tristessa is linked to the Kerouac canon in other ways as well. Kerouac writes in *Doctor Sax* that "memory and dream are intermixed in this mad universe," and dreams of his father, such as the one he mentions in *Tristessa,* appear throughout *Book of Dreams.* One may surmise that this opening passage of *Tristessa* is an instance of Kerouac's notorious "spontaneous prose," a rollicking, unfurling flash of prose only hinted at in *On the Road* and *The Dharma Bums,* a prose in which the whims of the moment carry sway in narrative direction. Kerouac includes the bit of the dream about his father simply because the memory of the dream flashed into his head as he was describing the scene with Tristessa. Weinreich points out that Kerouac repeats and thus revises the events when he writes about them. Kerouac's acts of repetition in his books represent these events "in the 'now,' in the present, in the truth of the moment—much as a jazzman blows the notes out of a horn." Weinreich concludes that the Duluoz Legend is a revision of those lived events, a "stylistic attempt to redefine legend" (Weinreich 12). Kerouac essentially revises the experience by repeating it in prose, creating a fresh "now" moment in the act of composition. There are instances when the circumstances of composition intrude directly onto the page. One can only see these breaks in the narrative as Kerouac's presence as a writer in the act of composition, a merging of the present moments of the recalled events and the event of composition. After all, Kerouac's moment is the moment of writing; he does not need to maintain the "willing suspension of disbelief" that ensures a reader's belief in a fictional world. Rather, his spontaneous prose style seems to insist that readers believe they are experiencing the text as it is being written, so Kerouac relies on a modified use of the suspension of disbelief; he welcomes readers to join him in the present moment. The Romantics, also masters of this technique, wished to create the sense of immediacy in writing as well.

The opening paragraph of *Tristessa* presents readers with a tangle of words and images that is a fresher, less revised example of Kerouac's artistic achievement in prose than much of what appears in *On the Road* or *The Dharma Bums*. Sound, sense, and apparent nonsense mingle in the prose. Some critics dismissed his efforts simply because of the rapid speed at which he frequently produced and the appearance of the prose on the page. One famous put-down came from Truman Capote, who said

Kerouac's work is merely typewriting. Kerouac later explained
to an interviewer that although the prose itself is written quickly,
the story germinates over time: "you think out what actually
happened, you tell friends long stories about it, you mull it over
in your mind, you connect it together at leisure, then when the
time comes to pay the rent again you force yourself to sit at the
typewriter, or at the writing notebook, and get it over with as fast
as you can . . . and there's no harm in that because you've got the
whole story lined up" (Berrigan 560).

Kerouac's spontaneous prose is characterized by long sentences that often are separated not by periods but by long
dashes. As Kerouac wrote to editor Robert Giroux in 1962, the
long dash gives the reader an advance visual signal that the sentence—its length based on breath—would be ending.[1] Kerouac
relates the written word tightly with the spoken word, and both
are yoked by the world of his mind as he sifts through dreams,
memories, and other various thought associations to build up
the sentences. In "Essentials of Spontaneous Prose" (1957)
Kerouac explains that instead of periods, he uses the long dash
to separate phrases based on breathing patters, as a jazz musician might phrase a solo. Kerouac also relied on the Bible for
justification of his spontaneous method. He cites Mark 13:11:
"Take no thought beforehand what ye shall speak, neither do ye
premeditate: but whatsoever shall be given you in that hour,
that speak ye: for it is not ye that speak, but the Holy Ghost"
("First Word" column, *Escapade* 1967). In *Desolation Angels*
Duluoz instructs a poet friend to achieve the best results by
writing "without stopping, without thinking, just go, I wanta
hear what's in the bottom of your mind" (128).

Kerouac's work was different from that of any contemporary American writer's; influenced by James Joyce, Marcel Proust, and jazz, he developed his own native American diction and his own method of layering meaning upon meaning. Shortly after finishing his first novel, *The Town and the City,* Kerouac knew that his approach had not come close enough to rendering reality on the pages. He told Cassady, "I have renounced fiction and fear. There is nothing to do but write truth" (*Letters* 248). In seeking to "write truth," Kerouac made difficult decisions that probably kept his work from being published for years. For one thing, he would no longer feel compelled to adhere to chronological storytelling: "Let's tear time up. Let's rip the guts out of reality" (*Letters* 274). Paradoxically, Kerouac implies that distortion of linear time and destruction of "reality" can approximate his vision more effectively than adherence to chronology and rationality. In fact, *On the Road* is strictly linear, but Kerouac's breakthrough in that book involves language and a thematic approach to time— breaking down normal awareness of the passage of time so that one may enter the "IT" of awareness. After this transitional book, Kerouac began writing the prose that he had been building toward for years.

In 1953, at the request of Ginsberg and Burroughs, Kerouac outlined the core features of his technique in a short piece called "Essentials of Spontaneous Prose," first published in *The Black Mountain Review*. The first section recalls the habit of Impressionist painters such as Cezanne and Renoir who lugged their palettes and easels out of the studios so that they could paint landscapes with immediacy and from direct observation.

Kerouac sought an immediate relation between the object and the writer. The prose that results from this relation is an unmediated representation in language that Kerouac suggests will be recognized by readers via a "telepathic shock." Besides the affinity this perspective shares with the Impressionists, Kerouac also shows his shared sense of human kinship with William Saroyan, one of his favorite writers of his youth. Kerouac naturally believed that a "telepathic shock" would be possible between the writer and the reader, an idea that goes against much postmodern American existential theory that holds that two people cannot possibly share the same wavelength of understanding. One reason for Kerouac's continued popularity as a writer may be the reality of that "telepathic shock" as many readers attest to the communication that takes place in his work between their minds and his. Whitman achieved no less when he stated in *Leaves of Grass,* "my soul embraces you this hour, and we affect each other without ever seeing each other." Kerouac sought in his work to find the wavelength that resonates the same for different people, a result he once referred to as "strokes of force never seen before and yet hauntingly familiar ([Edmund] Wilson's famous 'shock of recognition')" ("Are Writers Made or Born" 79).

For as many ways in which Kerouac and the Beat Generation artists were like the Impressionists, there are certainly many more ways in which they were different. Still, the comparison renders several key associations that help one understand that Kerouac was not simply a word-happy typist cranking out pages of unmediated flow. He focused on the obligations of the writer and the options that writers were currently pursuing. In a 1955 letter to his editor Malcolm Cowley, Kerouac admitted that he dissociated himself from analytical thinking and wrote as if he were reporting an endless dream. This report is the Duluoz Legend, unified, he claimed, by its spontaneous language (*Letters* 516). Kerouac also told Cowley that the only approach to writing is to be spontaneous; otherwise the result "can only be crafty and revised, by which the paradox arises, we get what a man has hidden, i.e. his craft, instead of what we need" (*Letters* 516). Kerouac valued the spontaneous riffs of jazz as applied to prose, but he most appreciated the rhythmic quality of the language he was producing. The most innovative jazz musicians understand the importance of exploring new musical ideas in the midst of their performances. They cannot say beforehand exactly what will happen in particular songs, but their musicianship, cultivated and evolved during long practice sessions, allows them to venture continually onto fresh ground. Their songs take on components of their immediate surroundings, their moods, and their interactions with other musicians.

In a later essay Kerouac may be supporting the merits of his artistic direction without mentioning himself by name: "A genius is simply a person who originates something never known before" ("Are Writers Made Or Born?" 79). Kerouac succeeds in making something new. Dissatisfied with the traditional narrative techniques that he proved a keen ability to produce (in *The Town and the City* or *The Dharma Bums,* for example), Kerouac plowed new turf for writers. The following chapters chart the path that he followed as he developed his ability to write prose, from his first book to his last. Each of the following chapters surveys Kerouac's progress and his artistic leaps and falls, too, as each new work presents its challenges.

CHAPTER THREE

The Town and the City (1950)

Kerouac's first novel is the result of a young artist attempting to express his vision of his contemporary post–World War II society. Kerouac faced a new, discordant, and paradoxically conformist and rebellious time, while his writer's tools enabled him only to capture his times in the traditional—though powerfully romantic and lyrical—mode of the past society. In appearance, his novel is everything a reader of the time would expect of an ambitious writer's first book. It is large, clamorous, packed with the observations of one flushed with excitement, and tempered with the too-complex world that rears in the present. *The Town and the City* stands as a testament to Kerouac's serious early efforts to be a great writer while serving as a touchstone of his ability at the end of the 1940s. It is a big book, one of the kind produced by writers who were avid readers in the 1930s, believing that the Great American Novel lurked in the crevices of her own doorways and dim neighborhoods, awaiting only the proper chemistry of mind, talent, audacity, insight, and subject matter to be brought into the light.

The book received generally tepid reviews and sold poorly, yet for nearly fifty years, owing to Kerouac's popularity with his other books, it has lingered on the bookstore shelves. Perhaps readers felt, as *The New Yorker* recommended in a 1950 review, that the book should be saved until there is absolutely nothing else to read. A more recent critic, Warren

French, claims that "such interest as the book possesses is the result of the very different body of work that the author subsequently signed Jack Kerouac" (25). French points out the book's differences from Kerouac's later work without apparently noticing the integral thematic unity the book shares with its later counterparts. Understanding *The Town and the City* is important in comprehending Kerouac. One cannot truly appreciate Kerouac and the complexity of the themes he would evolve throughout his career without reading his first book. Metaphorically, this novel is a mine that Kerouac would excavate in his subsequent books; it is also the lode of Kerouac's youthful experience and proficiency through age twenty-six, representing his all-out attempt to write the Great American Novel, to "explain everything to everybody" (*Vanity of Duluoz* 266). Most of Kerouac's important themes in his later work lie beneath the veneer of the Thomas Wolfe–like style. *On the Road, Doctor Sax, Maggie Cassidy, Book of Dreams, The Subterraneans, Visions of Gerard*—all incubate here awaiting Kerouac's artistic development for their release. The presence of Kerouac's wordplay early in his first book—"a starwealthy sky, Augustcool and calm" (20), for example—hints that conventional language and traditional novelistic formalities will not restrain him for long.

The Town and the City digs into the moods and motivations of an American family before and after World War II, using the Martin family as a microcosm for Kerouac's vision of the American condition. Despite the "hoodlum" reputation Kerouac would bear in the later 1950s, his first book is a sweet and gentle work for the most part, built on a series of family vignettes: the family goes to church and then opens gifts on Christmas Eve; a father and his youngest son spend a day at the horse race track; the kids pitch in to help one brother earn money to pay for a broken window; two of the brothers run away up the river for an adventure; one son rises to the status of a small-town hero in the big Thanksgiving Day football game. After Scribners rejected the novel, Kerouac wondered if his book was turned down because it is too full of simple pleasures, too full of family life; he feared that financially successful novels were constructed around maliciousness, while his family-centered story would be seen as too sentimental.[1]

The book begins with the town themes, modeled on a combination of Kerouac's own experiences and the big family and hometown of Thomas Wolfe, especially as chronicled in *Look Homeward, Angel.* The city life is the family fractured, and the bohemian characters Peter Martin encounters in New York are completely new—a crazy-minded underground quasi-criminal set who represent the "great molecular comedown" and "disintegrative decay" (370), the crashing of all that Peter had understood to be sacred and permanent and dependable about the family and the world he lived in. The upbeat tone established by the Martin father does not sustain the children as they mature into the postwar world. The collapse of the Martin family mirrors the disintegration of Kerouac's lost childhood innocence and the values that buttressed that life. In 1958 Warren Tallman described the collapse of trust, faith, certainty, and meaning into a "humpty dumpty heap,"[2] where being beat is a manner of survival. The word *bittersweet* best describes the notable flavor of the book, but the evocation is really of ominous and impending darkness, not bitterness. Kerouac sets such frequently repeated words as *gloom, brood, sad,* and *strange* against words with brighter connotations, such as *glee* and *gleam.* The image of reality reflected on water appears throughout the novel, with the unmistakable impression that for Kerouac the corporeal, the material, is ungraspable and ephemeral, but all the while truth lurks behind the image.

Contemporary critics generally have ignored *The Town and the City.* For one thing, it is the notorious "big book," one that contains the saga of a family as it evolves over several decades, quite unlike anything Kerouac ever attempted again.[3] In themselves, sheer bulk and scope should not deter a reader, but the book is not built upon any conventional adventure or plot to keep the reader intrigued. Instead it is an investigation of the interior family emotions and relationships as they would unfold in real life. Maybe, too, once Kerouac was notorious as the Beat Generation writer, his first novel seemed tame in subject and style, possessing a sound Tallman calls "soft music on a farther shore" (520). Kerouac himself referred to his style at this time as "the misty nebulous New England Idealist style" (*Vanity of Duluoz* 201) and later disparaged the "dreary" prose of the book (*The Subterraneans* 73). However, much is going on in this book too. Kerouac displays his writer's gifts as he sets scene after scene and shifts the pace and ambience of the writing appropriately. *The Town and the City* is a better book than critics generally give it credit for being, and ultimately it is significant in the Duluoz Legend for it unveils important themes that Kerouac would devote his career to developing.

The first sentence is the shortest sentence in the book: "The town is Galloway." That first sentence is just a warming up, a sound check, for the torrent of language that flows into the book, just as, in the second sentence, the Merrimack River flows into the narrative "out of endless sources and unfathomable springs" (3). The river represents life, the lives of the Galloway people, and especially the youngest Martin son, Mickey, who contemplates his own origins before he, like the Merrimack, one day "enters an infinity of waters and is gone" (3). The grown-ups generally exist on the surface levels of Galloway, but mysteries of life and the universe swirl around them, and if a man were to tune in, he would hear "something in the invisible brooding landscape surrounding the town, . . . [that] tells him a different story" (3). Discovering this "something" is Kerouac's goal in this book and perhaps in all his work. The ethereal, ghostly quality of this "something" interpenetrates the whole of *The Town and the City.*

The Martins' household is rock solid in the beginning of the story, a product of George Martin's keen American optimism and energy. George hustles from his printing business to the horse races to big cigars and suppers in the Chinese restaurant. He possesses the high-energy traits that attracted Kerouac throughout his career. George is gregarious and engaging and boisterous—a "man's man" who is seen about town in restaurants and back-room poker games (8). George's vitality is sufficient to bolster the family against the weight of various family troubles in the children's youthful years, but his vivacity and endurance are no match for the instability that arrives when they become old enough to face life on their own in a world that has grown unrecognizable from the one through which George moves so confidently.

In a contrast to George's buoyant determination, Kerouac imbues his first book with a hazy and mysterious romanticism that seeps from page to page, giving the book a sweet-but-sad tone. This tone is an aspect of Romantic melancholy, a longing for *le temps perdu* as in Wolfe and Proust. For example, the following phrases appear throughout: "something strangely tragic, something beautiful forever" (7); "something dark, warlike, mournful and far" (238); "something complete, and wise, and brutal too" (360); "something gleeful, rich and dark, something rare and wildly joyful" (411); "something furiously sad, angry, mute, and piteous" (443); "something undiscoverably beautiful and now gone" (458).

Peter and other characters to a lesser extent feel the pressure to express some unsayable message, to embrace all of reality, to occupy the same experience; in short, he yearns to convey effectively the brotherhood of man, but he cannot. When he meets his girlfriend in New York City, he is despondent because he cannot tell her everything that has happened to him. Peter possesses, as later Kerouac characters will as well, a pervasive sadness made more poignant by his inability to express it, to share his insights with others. (379). Kerouac later recalled that his youthful determination in writing *The Town and the City* stemmed from his yearning to recount, and thereby salvage, the difficult life he had lived to that point (*Vanity of Duluoz* 268). *The Town and the City,* and maybe his whole opus, is Kerouac's attempt to succeed where Peter failed.

The novel is mostly a boy's story, focusing on brothers Joe, Francis, and Peter. The story opens in 1935, when Joe is seventeen, Francis is just beginning high school, and Peter is thirteen. The book ends in 1946, when Peter is twenty-four and on the road alone, hitchhiking west. When George loses his printing business, he accepts a variety of jobs to keep his family together. The Martins move to New York City—thus the title of the book—and gradually the family members disperse with no new children carrying on the family name of Martin. Quite early in the novel, young Mickey Martin has an epiphany of the sort that Kerouac records throughout his novels: a moment when one forgets who one is and why one is there. Instead, there is only the flash of awareness that outside of their mothers' protective and loving embrace, all children must suddenly face loneliness (15). Kerouac reflects in *On the Road* that people suffer in life to regain an elusive rapture they may have known in their mothers' wombs (124). Boosterism, good spirits, looking forward hopefully, giving it the old college try: none of these classic American optimisms could save George and protect his family. The Martin children mature and see their parents as fumbling human beings, after all; and in the larger scheme that Kerouac merges into the family tale, the modern world no longer follows what the fathers of the last generation knew. Francis, too, realizes that adults—and specifically his father—misled children about the nature of the world they would grow into (157).

In Kerouac's next book, *On the Road,* he will take up this theme again: "Isn't it true that you start your life a sweet child believing in everything under your father's roof? Then comes the day of the Laodiceans, when you know you are wretched and miserable and poor and blind and naked" (105). Like Laodicea, the once-great and boastful city of Bible times that disappeared in the Middle Ages, Galloway and its sense of place as an American refuge too falls away. Jesus attacks the pride of the Laodiceans in Revelation 3:14, pointing out that their condition is always precarious: "For you say, I am rich, I have prospered, and I need nothing; not knowing that you are wretched, pitiable, blind, and naked." The loss of the father's world, then, is one major theme in *The Town and the City* and in Kerouac's subsequent work.

Peter Martin's sentiments parallel Kerouac's own elation and vision as a young artist and present his motivation for writing the novel. Peter wants to speak with his fellow footballers and break through the tough, masculine exteriors they present to each other. He longs to express a common understanding they each shared, to bring them somehow to a point of spiritual and emotional camaraderie that would supplant the merely physical teamship they exhibit on the football field (127). Nevertheless, Peter cannot pierce the barriers of socially imposed behaviors. Peter does find a brotherly rapport with Alex Panos, based on Sammy Sampas, "the curly-headed little Greek kid on the sandbank" (133) who embodies Saroyan's vision of human brotherhood. Alex propounds the essential message that humanity is one great family and repeats a call to "the brotherhood of man," a transcendent socialism. There is the great human family, yet its most obvious demonstration is the nuclear family itself, which falls apart throughout the novel. Joe's final scene in the novel suggests that children can rebuild families, though—new renditions of the old, full of new episodes. On the other hand, Francis, in his decadence, severs all the connections he has had with his father.

As the novel develops, two main relationships emerge, one between Peter and his father and one between Francis and Peter. Francis is older than Peter and more jaded. While Peter becomes an impressive football player who ships out with the merchant marine and later meets a gang of bohemians in New York, Francis thinks of Berkeley, California, "real intellectuals" (116), and life in a sophisticated (and ultimately decadent) setting. Warren French makes an excellent study of the dichotomy in Kerouac's own character, based on the distinctions between Peter and Francis. French finds that "'Peter' and 'Francis' must have warred constantly for domination over Kerouac's thoughts and actions, and this struggle was to play a major role in the shaping of the Duluoz Legend" (28).

The two brothers most clearly contrast their relationship in two conversations. The first occurs during Peter's first-year Christmas visit. Peter had decided already that the formal education offered by the university falls short of affecting him spiritually and emotionally (147), an awareness that matches Kerouac's own during his first year of school. Besides, Peter dismissed the university's teachings in favor of "his own kind of people" of the towns he knew and valued. Peter maintains "that you can't explain the world," while Francis does not "believe in mysteries" (155). Peter tries to illustrate that people of the world are real and sincere, a point Kerouac, like William Saroyan, spent his career attempting to prove. Peter's appreciation for the apparent simplicity of the town's holiday atmosphere does not engage Francis, who says that Peter's simple, pure vision of reality involves only the daytime: for Francis, the ravaging, destructive effects of the night overpower any life-bringing qualities associated with the day (156).

Years later Peter and Francis have another conversation the weekend of their father's funeral. They go fishing with their oldest brother, Joe, the three brothers reunited by the event of their father's death. As they observe a hooked fish struggling in the shallow water, Peter brings up their earlier discussion. Peter feels like the fish, "chained to the mystery of his own dumb incomprehension" (494), and he asks how one is to persevere in the presence of suffering (495). Francis and Joe regard Peter with warmth and kindness, comprehending somehow that he had brought their mutual feelings to light through his child-like apprehension of their individual sorrows (496). Thus Peter makes good on his prep-school wish to share an understanding with his fellows, to break through their veneer of personality to a common necessary faith beneath, and that too is Kerouac's goal in this book. Kerouac's Saroyanesque humanity shows his compassion for people and opens the door for his yet-developing ability to write for a generation, to encompass the shared sensitivity among the many. Kerouac wrote to Neal Cassady as he worked on *The Town and the City,* "I refuse to believe that anyone in the world is not of my own feather, really, in the long run, I refuse to believe it with vanity, unhappiness, and longing. Life must be rich and full of loving" (*Letters* 117). This statement underpins a principal Kerouac characteristic and is the key to what he meant by "Beat Generation."

The notes on the first-edition book jacket describe *The Town and the City* as "one of the most moving father-son narratives ever written." When Peter tries to explain his inner desires to his father, George exclaims that his son is too involved with words to understand the implications behind them. Ultimately this is one important distinction between the father, a man tied to the things of the world, and the son who possesses a vision but not the ability to express it. The discussions between Peter and his father in the kitchen sound like exchanges of a generation-gap debate. George allows that Peter's generation understands but does not value the difference between right and wrong (409). Later George criticizes Peter's new friends from the city, the friends that Kerouac based on his own real-life friends who would become the core of the Beat Generation, claiming that Peter's new crowd included drug addicts and lawbreakers (420). Peter searches for the term to describe some Times Square characters who interested him: "I don't know what you call them— they're just waiting around for something" (420). An authentic hipster, Junkey, says, "Don't you know, I'm beat" (402), and Kerouac's catchy phrase for labeling his generation is nearly in place. The novel concludes with a quartet of deaths. Waldo Meister, one of Peter's city friends, kills himself; Alexander Panos, Peter's childhood poet friend, is killed in the war in Italy; George dies; and little brother Charley is killed in Okinawa. In George's last days Peter comes to understand that life is made up of love and work and hope, and these three are interdependent.

Kerouac reveals in his letters and elsewhere that Thomas Wolfe woke him to the idea of America as a subject in itself, not as merely a geography where the struggles of life go on. Kerouac constructs huge complex "cycloramas," or observations of America's war preparation. Kerouac tries to capture the manifold activities of everyone at once, like those photograph books that feature pictures from all over the country at the same moment. Peter adapts to postwar America by making new friends, including nineteen-year-old Leon Levinsky, a character Kerouac modeled on Allen Ginsberg. Levinsky insists that simplicity has been lost—that instead the modern world is both complex and evil (368). He is writing a poem about "an evil magician surrounded by the decline of the West," borrowing from the title of the Oswald Spengler book—*The Decline of the West*—that interested the Beat writers. Levinsky also refers to the disfigured and diseased patrons of the Nickle-O, a Times Square amusement center, as "children of the sad American paradise" and identifies post-atom-bomb, early-cold-war paranoia. Although Peter denies that everyone has become deformed, guilty of inner shame, he does admit that some essential qualities of the country have changed since the war (370).

Although not his best book, *The Town and the City* is a strong first book, and Kerouac had the chance to work out the major themes and motifs that would remain imbedded in the Duluoz Legend. Kerouac shows also in his first novel his facility with a Wolfe-like blend of poetry and prose: "In time, all was infolded in the earth again, in the glee of home again" (34). At times Kerouac brings the darkness of gloom and the brightness of glee together: "Peter ran through the streets, jubilant with doom" (300). One gets the impression that Kerouac, like Francis in the story, sometimes "chuckled as though somewhat overcome by the sound of the words" (154). In Kerouac's subsequent books the sounds of words became so prominent that he would sometimes sacrifice the sense of words. Kerouac also introduces one of his most enduring images, the neon on red-brick walls: "the old brown boxcars standing in the darkness by grimy redbrick warehouses, the cheap hotel with its red neon" (232). Kerouac will bring this image to fuller use in *Visions of Cody* and later books as a neon promise of Saturday night excitement runs abruptly into the redbrick harshness of reality.

Kerouac's first published novel also represents his first significant interactions with the business of publishing, and the lessons he learned would determine the way he worked with agents and editors in his professional future. For one thing, he later complained that Robert Giroux, his editor, turned *The Town and the City* "from a great book into a good novel, then said: 'This is not a poetic age'" (*Some of the Dharma* 128). Kerouac also complained in letters to friends that Giroux's cuts reduced the depth and poignancy of the book. His manuscript of *The Town and the City* numbers over eleven hundred pages, and the published book contains roughly two-thirds of that material. One element that Giroux cut included the episodes of the Martin sisters; little of their stories remains.

The themes and episodes of later Kerouac novels are suggested first in the pages of *The Town and the City.* For example, as in *On the Road,* springtime brings the need for traveling. Joe vows to travel across America just for adventure's sake and wishes he had "lived in those days when you rode on horseback and all you had ahead of you was this unexplored space, the wide open spaces" (*Town* 68). Little Mickey wants to go along, but like Sal in *On the Road,* his notions of life in the West are based on popular films. Alexander complains to Peter about "Time! Time!": "There are so many things to learn, to do, and time rushes past!" (180). Dean Moriarty will finally show Sal how to cope with the unceasing passage of time. Kerouac uses the same phrases in both works: "forlorn rags" (*Town* 251; *Road* 310) and "All I do is die!" (*Town* 281; *Road* 181). He even uses the phrase "sad American paradise" (369), which prefigures the name Sal Paradise. After Kerouac finished *On the Road* and its counterpart, *Visions of Cody,* he wrote *Doctor Sax,* another book whose theme *The Town and the City* adumbrates. Twice Kerouac mentions the Martin kids' fascination with *The Shadow* magazine, a basis for Doctor Sax. In *The Town and the City* Doctor Sax already roams Kerouac's half-lit streets, and though he is yet unnamed, Kerouac is aware of his presence: "In the smoky air of evening now, there was something, mad with glee, something that laughed in a soundless choking in the dark" (171). *Maggie Cassidy,* too, first appears here—as Mary, who bewitches Francis. And although he does not yet know of the Buddhist deities who will prowl his northwestern mountaintops, Kerouac can already uncork the prose ability that later will allow him to describe the raging landscapes of his pinnacle lookout in *Desolation Angels* (*Town* 304). Like the Kerouacs, the Martins lost a young son, a situation Kerouac explores fully in *Visions of Gerard.* These passages and the major motifs demonstrate that though stylistically distinct, *The Town and the City* is of a piece with Kerouac's entire oeuvre. Although this book appeared more than seven years before the publication of Kerouac's next novel, Kerouac never stopped writing, and many tales and important themes that he produced in the coming years hover within this title. Though it is the work of a writer not yet fully developed, this book is definitely of the cloth from which Kerouac would cut the Duluoz Legend.

CHAPTER FOUR

On the Road (1957)

Paperback book reprints of *On the Road* call the book "The Classic Novel of the Beat Generation," a claim that deserves scrutiny. Literary critics raise few eyebrows now when the epithet *classic* is attached to this book. Yet publishers rejected the novel for seven years as unliterary or loosely structured, and many critics attacked the book with rancor upon its publication. The term *novel,* too, is problematic, for the story traces, with few variations, the actual events that actual people experienced. Readers wonder whether this is a work of fiction or an (auto)biographical work. Kerouac has achieved a reputation for blunt honesty, for putting it down the way it happened. Kerouac once told biographer Ann Charters that he had written the book for his new wife, "to tell her what I'd been through."[1] Kerouac's friend John Clellon Holmes reports that Kerouac had vowed to "write it down as fast as I can, exactly like it happened."[2] In its elevation of life for the sake of art, the book lingers somewhere between truth and artifice.[3] Then there is the whole circus of the Beat Generation, a group that may have been limited to a half-dozen member artists who interacted intensely in the late 1940s—and who are written about in this book—or perhaps a group that ten years later included every unshaven "beatnik" who disdained mainstream American work life for banging bongos and scrawling poems in notebooks in coffeehouses. This is to say that Kerouac's most famous novel comes with many associations that work to inform and mislead the reader before the cover is opened. The book is both a story and a cultural event.

After finishing *The Town and the City,* Kerouac changed as a writer. Thomas Wolfe had influenced his language and style as he approached the thematic matter of his first book. Now Kerouac sought the proper expression for his road experiences. Although he worked on his road book for several years, he was dissatisfied with the results. Extant manuscripts and letters to friends make it clear that at first he was continuing in much the same style as he had written *The Town and the City.* William Burroughs had begun to write by this time, and Kerouac had read his first manuscript, *Junkie,* and was impressed with the matter-of-fact, Dashiell Hammett–like style. Burroughs dubbed his no-nonsense approach to writing "factualism." Kerouac picked up on the straight-ahead style and Burroughs's ideas of the dominance of American law enforcement.

Almost since the date of its publication, Kerouac readers have speculated about the famous scroll of paper that Kerouac ran through his typewriter as he produced his most famous book. Some critics have suggested that if the original typescript were unveiled, readers might have access to a work with a greater stylistic achievement than what was published. Even before the book's publication, rumors circulated for years that Viking editors had hacked away at the prose, sacrificing Kerouac's loose, jazzy, and inspired writing for the sake of readers—and thus better sales. Kerouac's initial submission of his *On the Road* scroll to Robert Giroux of Harcourt, Brace is a well-known literary anecdote. According to the general version of the story, Kerouac finished speed-typing his novel in three weeks in spring 1951 and, in a fit of exuberance, rushed to his editor's office and unfurled the scroll with a flourish. Robert Giroux responded unsympathetically—"How can we edit a thing like that?"—and Kerouac, utterly sensitive to the altering of his words, stormed out of the office, not to see Giroux again for several years. Sometime after that, as the story goes, Malcolm Cowley, a chronicler of the Lost Generation, championed Kerouac's novel at Viking. After much cutting, consolidating of episodes, and rewriting over the course of six years, the reading public finally got the bible of the Beat Generation, and Kerouac belatedly became an overnight sensation.

Mythical stories are often more absorbing than the truth. In Kerouac's case, the facts may never entirely be known. Essentially, it seems evident that Kerouac, a hundred-words-per-minute typist, taped a series of art-paper sheets together and trimmed the edge so the resulting scroll would fit into his typewriter. This way he could type quickly without having to interrupt his flow to put in fresh sheets of regular typing paper. The scroll typescript is now in conservation in the New York Public Library, where it is in fragile condition. In 1995 it was on display there under a glass case. The scroll is the width of regular typing paper, wound like a roll of paper towels around a spool. The scroll measures some five inches in diameter, and the first foot was unrolled so that visitors could read the opening, single-spaced typed lines. The text begins this way: "I first met Neal not long after my father died . . . I had just gotten over a serious illness that I won't bother to talk about except that it really had something to do with my father's death and my awful feeling that everything was dead. With the coming of Neal there really began for me that part of my life that you could call my life on the road." Kerouac produced the reportedly 120-foot-long typescript in three weeks of steady typing. This typescript is the raw material out of which Kerouac's critical and popular reputations were formed; to trace its history is to trace the development of a professional career. Kerouac wrote at least twenty books, but *On the Road* established his character in the eyes of early critics and readers alike. The packaging of that book—from rough scroll to Viking bestseller—is the packaging of Kerouac as he became a salable commodity and a literary figure.

By late spring 1951 Kerouac had already retyped the scroll onto regular sheets, and the result was a 450-page typescript. During that initial retyping session, and over the next six years, Kerouac had many opportunities to revise and cut the text. Apparently the changes that he made at Viking's request came mostly in the form of cuts, insertions, punctuation changes, and the alterations of characters to hide their real-life identities. Whether or not Malcolm Cowley or another Viking editor "made endless revisions and inserted thousands of needless commas" (Berrigan 540), as Kerouac later asserted, is still a matter of contention. Cowley stated clearly that such was not the case: "Jack and his memory are very, very unfair to me. Blaming me for putting in or taking out commas and caps and what-not in *On the Road*" (Gifford and Lee 206). An excerpt from *On the Road* published in *New World Writing* in April 1955 gives readers an opportunity to see what the prose of the book may have looked like before Viking's editing. Titled

"Jazz of the Beat Generation," the excerpt corresponds to approximately ten pages of *On the Road* and employs forty fewer commas. For example, the phrase "raised the horn and blew high wide and screaming" appears in *On the Road* as "raised the horn and blew high, wide, and screaming" (197). What matters the most to readers who wish to understand Kerouac's continuing development as a prose stylist, though, is his judgment that the scroll version of *On the Road* contained his and Cassady's adventures written in a style he would soon abandon.

The story is simple; two young men travel the American continent looking outwardly for kicks and inwardly for salvation. In late 1946 Sal Paradise, a young man from the East despondent after the breakup of his marriage, meets Dean Moriarty (based on Neal Cassady), a young man from the West who had spent much of his youth in reform schools and who, via his tremendous enthusiasm for life, stirs up a belief in Sal in renewal and the possibility of adventure. Early in the novel Sal goes from feeling that "everything was dead" to believing in a fresh start: he is "beginning to get the bug like Dean" (6). When Dean returns West in the spring, Sal pledges to follow him, but his naive notions of travel on his initial hitchhiking trip lead only to a rainy night along a lonely road. Sal's naive viewpoint is one important thematic element in the novel.

In Chicago, Sal listens to bop, and he realizes that all of America is a kind of "backyard" where his friends are scattered but wrapped up in the same concerns. Kerouac had used the image of rain to unite separate people in *The Town and the City,* and he would use rain throughout his writings. In *On the*

Road, however, no other image so successfully gathers the loose threads of his relationships as does the jazz to which they all listen and with which they identify. Jazz is the beating heart of *On the Road.* His perception of his friends scattered across the continent (14) sets up the loose structure the book has—Sal runs from one group to another just to see what will happen—and it also establishes the roots of the Beat Generation that the book spread. That is, Sal's friends represent a peculiar subset of the demographic group who came of age during World War II and are now coping in its aftermath.

Part 2 of the novel takes up more than a year later. Sal observes that Dean has gained confidence and maturity (114). Sal begins to see into Dean's mystical nature: "'You can't make it with geometry and geometrical systems of thinking. It's all *this*!' [Dean] wrapped his finger in his fist; the car hugged the line straight and true" (120). Dean frantically attempts to explain to Sal his notions of "IT," a metaphysical breakthrough that cancels the ravaging effects of time. The pursuit of "IT" is another important thematic element in the novel. When Sal returns to New York, in part 5, he finally meets the woman he will marry. Dean hits the road again while Sal stays home, wondering about the meaning of their travels but somehow more secure in his feelings about America and its people (309). All the trips that Sal outlines in his narrative begin to affect readers as details from various trips blur, origins and destinations are forgotten, and the going itself is the only moment.

On the Road begins at the beginning, so to speak, following the tradition of many mythic and epic narratives: "I first met Dean not long after my wife and I split up" (3). In fact, the story occurs entirely between the narrator's split from his first wife and his meeting with the woman who would become his second wife, the woman for whom he ostensibly searches throughout the novel (306). Women in American literature frequently represent the imposition of civilizing influences over the frontier-pushing males. Although Dean and Sal pursue women during their voyages across the American landscape, Dean refuses to commit himself to a mature relationship while Sal seems to understand the need for a civilizing influence: he wishes for a wife with whom he can share a peaceful life and leave behind the "franticness" of his youth wih Dean (116). Much of the novel plays off the tension between Sal's sentimental notion of a woman as nurturing wife and Dean's image of a woman as sexual object.

From this perspective, the novel presents Sal Paradise as a young man—he describes himself as "a college boy" several times—who sows his wild oats between commitments to women and marriage, which represent a conventional counterpoint to his seemingly fatuous life on the road. Sal's friends frequently ask him why he is going on the road, and he never has a comfortable answer. On his first trip a carnival operator offers Sal a job and asks, "You boys going somewhere, or just going?" Sal muses, "We didn't understand his question, and it was a damned good question" (22). This uncertainty follows Sal throughout his travels. Either Sal is on a quest or he is simply moving, leaving behind confusion and creating certainty and order in the very act of compulsion, riding the "protective road" of anonymity (223). There may be no sensible reason whatever for Sal to go on the road except that he is a writer in search of material. He admits early in the novel that Dean will abandon him when he is nearly destitute, yet he will forgive Dean (11), for Sal hungers for experience to feed his desire to write. The final justification for his coast-to-coast excursions is the novel that results from those experiences. Sal confesses that he himself is not nearly as interesting as the characters who intrigue him: "I shambled after as I've been doing all my life after people who interest me" (8), and he is a "lout compared" (7) to his friends. When Dean and Carlo Marx, launch into all-night conversations in which they seek to share their souls, Sal goes to sleep, asking only to be kept apprised of events as they unfold (50). In fact, many of his utterances create a kind of fugue on this theme: "we followed sheepishly" (114); "I only went along for the ride, and to see what else Dean was going to do" (129); "I didn't want to interfere, I just wanted to follow" (132); "I am always ready to follow Dean" (262). In *Desolation Angels* the narrator regards a passenger who "has taken the back seat in life, to watch and be interested (like me)" (94). In *Visions of Cody* Duluoz observes that "Cody just runs the machine, I sit and meditate Cody and the machine both" (138). In this passive role Sal Paradise gains fuel for writing as the car burns fuel on the road. Sal realizes early that Dean is conning him, as Dean cons many characters throughout the book, but Sal uses his own subterfuge as he gains material for the book he will write at the end of the adventures, after he settles into his home with his new woman. Dean disappears into the turmoil of his American life, while Sal settles down and profits, literally, from the experience. The road leaves Sal with a tangible accomplishment.

Yet this conclusion is too simple, for there is other evidence that Sal needs his road experience for entirely different reasons. At the beginning of the book Sal is not only naive (he imagines one straight line of road that will take him into the West of his movie-and-book-inspired imagination), he is also listless and enervated, believing that his surroundings were lifeless (3) and his college experience was unproductive (10). Dean represents possibilities, open-ended adventure, an escape from the decadence of Sal's sullen hipster friends in New York City. Dean offers a sunlit future, a positive force, a chance to be a man in the great western sense of cowboys and frontiersmen. Dean also reminds Sal of his younger self, of a playmate of his childhood when times were simple and joy-filled, and in Dean's voice Sal hears the familiar calls of his schoolboy friends in his old neighborhood, in an idyllic past he longs to regain (10). Dean is both a call to Sal's childhood past and to his future that will be free of the "tedious intellectualness," slinking criminality, and negativity of his current crowd. Dean is a natural man, comfortable and genuine in a way that Sal admires and envies. By saddling up with Dean, Sal is sure that in his future "there'd be girls, visions, everything; somewhere along the line the pearl would be handed to me" (11). So Sal cannot lose; he will encounter the vivifying ordeals of life at Dean's pace, and the result will be a more comprehensive life and a new book.

Kerouac wrote this novel in the spring of 1951, one year after the publication of *The Town and the City*. Sal, as narrator, intensifies the naiveté of his earlier self. The earlier self, young Sal, is busy writing his first book. The stages of Sal's composition of his first unnamed novel separate *On the Road* into sections:

- Dean initially comes to Sal since mutual friends told him Sal is a writer—in fact Dean witnesses Sal at work at the typewriter and cheers him on;
- Sal goes west for the first time ostensibly so that he can earn enough money to finish his book, and one job that Remi lines up for him is as a Hollywood scriptwriter;
- Sal's return to his "half-finished manuscript" (107) ends part 1;
- part 2 begins "over a year later" (109) after Sal has finished his book;
- the book's acceptance provides Sal the financial opportunity to invite Dean to travel to Italy (189), though part 3 ends with the trip canceled;
- part 4 begins with Sal traveling west with money from the sale of his book;
- and the book ends when Sal settles down to write the road story, his next book.

Kerouac essentially retells the history of the composition of his first book as he writes the second one. This overlap allows Kerouac to examine the close ties between pure experience and experience for the sake of art. The narrator's regard for his own work has deeper significance for Kerouac; for the first time in his "fiction" Kerouac writes about the subject of writing. In later work this reflexivity is often at the core of his writing. On the other hand, Dean writes nothing until the end of the novel, "a huge letter eighteen thousand words long" (306), while Sal writes continuously and makes good on his investment in the road experiences. Yet the hero of *On the Road* is really Dean, the one who cuts closest to reality, who is utterly involved in his life as he lives it, who moves in rhythm from moment to moment, admonishing his friends to forgive and forget, to understand that, in his often repeated motto, "Everything is always all right!" Sal rarely achieves this level of detachment; implicit in the story is the notion that his eye roves not solely for "eyeball kicks" but for details to record in his book.

Kerouac altered his own biography so he could downplay Sal's role and establish the first-person narrator as a shambling, naive figure who can fade to the background when Dean takes the stage. Sal's innocence and lack of sophistication do not necessarily mirror Kerouac's life either. Kerouac had been in the merchant marine during World War II and had gone on trips to Iceland and Liverpool. In addition, he had been a football hero and had been elected president of the sophomore class at Columbia. Although Sal mentions briefly that he had been to sea (28) and received benefits of the GI bill (179), there are no other indications that he was as widely traveled or as savvy as Kerouac was when he lived Sal's adventures. Again, the book stands on its own as a novel (or a "true-story novel," as Kerouac once referred to his work), yet seeing the adjustments that Kerouac made offers insight into his technique. Sal is wide-eyed and open to the new adventures that Dean promises, and at the end of the book Sal is more jaded and cynical, yet experienced and ready to get off the road and on to the task of writing. Sal claims early in the novel that "the things that were to come are too fantastic not to tell" (9), a classic impulse to justify any kind of writing. Yet the significance of the experiences that were "too fantastic" are undercut as ends in themselves. As Sal reveals at the beginning of the novel, the adventures will end and Dean will be ultimately sad and tired (8). Sal's outcome suggests that Dean's path may be a fine one to travel *for a time* since one can reap the benefits of the road experience and then transfer those benefits to an accomplishment such as writing.

Fathers, in their absence, represent an important theme in *On the Road. The Town and the City* ends with the father's funeral and his son Peter heading out on the road. Kerouac's original scroll manuscript of *On the Road* begins "I first met Neal not long after my father died," a beginning that links the two books as parts of a series and that matches Kerouac's biography. Sal never mentions his mother[4] and mentions his father only obliquely, when a racehorse named Big Pop reminds him of his father. Dean's "folks" were on the road when Dean was born, setting up his footloose life, but his mother died before Dean ever knew her, and his hobo father, Old Dean Moriarty the Tinsmith, is lost somewhere in America. Dean's father looms invisibly over the story, presenting a warning of an ominous possible future for Dean himself—or for any road goer. In fact, Dean once speculates that he and Sal may end up old bums together (251). Old Dean appears in references at least a dozen times; yet like Hamlet's father's ghost, he is always distant and hazy, his meaning unclear. The bum's life may be one of joy, freedom, and lazy, starry nights, selling makeshift flyswatters door-to-door to make money for wine (207). Perhaps, though, Old Dean's life may be more as Sal imagines it, living the hobo's life of freedom along the rails but dying finally in poverty and loneliness (132).

Other offstage fathers are mentioned in the story, always by the sons who are active characters. On Sal's first trip west, he rides with two farm boys who travel with permission from "their old men" (24). Even Montana Slim, a road bum with a sneaky look, sends a postcard to his father, an act that allows Sal to see Slim's tender side. Finally, though, the idea of fatherhood has deeper significance for Sal. On their trip into the wilds of Mexico, Sal finds the Fellahin Indians, who possess in Sal's eyes a fundamental, uncultivated naturalness and who are the fathers of mankind (280–81). Kerouac suggests that sometime in the faraway past, people lived in harmony with nature in the Garden of Eden. In the middle of the twentieth century, people live in ignorance and suffering, out of joint with their times. Kerouac repeats this theme in different ways in this book and throughout his writing. Every joyous moment in *On the Road* ends up in disappointment and regret. Every big night precedes a painful "morning after." One continual refrain is the collapse that follows bliss, and so each event can be seen in its entirety as a fall from the Garden. Achieving "IT" can allay the grief and forestall doom, but "IT" by nature is ever elusive, like the "something" that permeates *The Town and the City*.

In order to re-enter the Garden of Eden Sal would bond to the people of the earth, and this desire partly makes up his reasons for travel. Dean is an outcast nearly everywhere he goes. Nonetheless, Dean claims that he knows the people, that he can subsist in the American culture. Most observers believe, though, that his methods are those of a con man. Although

there are many instances of Sal's own sense of being an outcast, he focuses mostly on racial issues. Sal seeks the "beat"
genuineness that he believes nonwhite races possess in America. In their first adventure together, Sal is eager to go with
Dean to meet "two colored girls" (7). The two girls do not show
up; this is but the first of their plans that fall through. Yet more
important, Sal does not hesitate to cross the border between
white and black. Nor does Sal hesitate to ride on a flatbed truck
with hoboes. He identifies with them though he has a home to
which he can return and money for which he can wire. His
association with hoboes is complete when he meets the "Ghost
of the Susquehanna" and claimes that they were bums together
(104). One result of Sal's empathy is that he moves outside
mainstream American society and finds greater meaning in the
singularity of those who do not follow in conformist patterns.
Kerouac once wrote that he was neither American nor Euro-
pean; instead he felt like an Inidan exile (*Letters* 381).

In Los Angeles, Sal meets a Mexican girl named Terry and
establishes with her a kind of surrogate marriage as they spend
more than two weeks together "for better or worse" (85). Terry
is the perfect companion for Sal; he will discover as the story
progresses that he needs more than white America offers him.
He treasures bop jazz, especially that of black musicians Char-
lie Parker, Miles Davis, Willie Jackson, and Lester Young. On
subsequent trips he develops the conviction that his white heritage has been a hindrance to his spiritual development. In fact,
as an Italian, Sal can sometimes blend with the Mexican popu-
lation as he picks cotton and sleeps in a tent, becoming "a man
of the earth" until he forgets, for a time, his travels and his

friends (97). When Sal is away from Dean and picks cotton with Terry, he likens himself to an "old Negro" (97). When a group of "Okies" mistake him for a Mexican, he comments, "in a way, I am" (97).[5]

On a later trip Sal spends several lonely evenings in Denver. Sal grasps that it is his heritage that deserts him and wishes that he were "a Negro" because his existence as a white man had not brought him "enough life, joy, kicks, darkness, music, not enough night" (180). He longs to "exchange worlds with the happy, true-hearted, ecstatic Negroes of America" (180). Sal's empathy is admirable, even if his whimsy seems a bit naive. Warren Tallman writes that outcasts in America in the 1940s, such as Negroes, had been forced to accept the futility of integration into society as a whole. Instead, they inhabit a "social purgatory." Tallman suggests that one way these outcasts cope is by giving up their egos and falling back not upon the mercy of society but into the moment, an existence entirely in the "now." To survive there, they must learn to "swing": "To swing is to enter into full alliance with the moment and to do this is to triumph over the squares who otherwise run the world" (515–16). Kerouac's spontaneous prose, derived in part from the improvisational nature of bop, would be the vehicle that transports him through the present, from moment to moment. In his desires to escape his "whiteness," Sal continually returns to the essence of his own nature. He cannot change his ethnicity, but through empathy and the writer's descriptive power he succeeds in moving—for a time—in other worlds. Like Natty Bumppo, Sal is uncomfortable in his own civilization but provides a bridge between it and other "less civilized" ways of life. One value of this book is that Kerouac shows that despite the surface differences among the various "outsiders" he knows, deep human affinities endure. As much as anything else, this awareness may be at the core of what he meant by "beat."

The word or a variation of the word *beat*[6] appears a dozen or so times in the novel. Initially *beat* is an adjective that describes Eddie's sweater (18); Sal also refers to the "old bums and beat cowboys of Larimer Street" (37); Dean says that his eyes are "red, sore, tired, beat" (50); and so on. *Beat* has its most important uses, though, when Sal describes the more spiritual aspects the term connotes. Sal sees Carlo and Dean as representatives of a type, of "the sordid hipsters of America, a new beat generation that [he] was slowly joining" (54). In a climactic scene, Sal becomes aware of Dean's spiritual success in coping with his lot in life. Thrown out by his wife, Dean has just faced the scourge of friends who charge him with irresponsibility and lack of seriousness. For Sal, Dean is illuminated as "the HOLY GOOF" (194). Dean does not try to extricate himself from these charges. Instead, he endures and escapes into the moment with all its potent and apocalyptic vibrations, accepting all that surrounds him with a series of affirmations, until finally, "he was BEAT—the root, the soul of Beatific" (195). The Oxford English Dictionary defines *beatitude*—a term Kerouac knew well—as "Supreme blessedness or happiness," and this meaning is significant here. Dean has hit the lowest point, yet paradoxically this is also a peak of understanding. The refusals on all sides to accept him have left him utterly destitute, not only from home and love life but even from friendship and understanding. One may draw a connection to the Beatitudes, the declarations made by Jesus in the Sermon on the Mount, Matthew, chapter 5, that begins, "Blessed are the poor in spirit, for theirs is the kingdom of heaven." Only Sal, who always defends Dean, grasps the importance of the insights Dean has.

Sal can be truly sympathetic because even though his life has been much more stable than Dean's, he has had visions of his own. When Dean and Marylou abandon him on the West Coast, Sal experiences a moment of epiphany (173). Kerouac drew this experience from his own life. As he explained in a letter to Cassady, whole episodes of a past life flooded him while he stood transfixed. The moment meant more than a past life revealed, however. Kerouac tells Cassady that he felt "heavenly rapture" followed by the "contemplation of rapture (which is beatitude)." The significance came in his realization that, had he been prepared to receive the vision, he would achieve an understanding of God that would bring salvation, a moment set up even by Kerouac's choice of his narrator's name, Salvatore Paradise (*Letters* 278). This could have been Kerouac's great disappearing act, when he could dissolve his ego and blend into the totality of creation, to swing with the moment. Like Jackie Duluoz listening to Doctor Sax's speech but not fathoming it, Sal can only sigh that he is not mature enough yet to benefit from the vision (173).

One of the keys to *On the Road*'s continuing popularity is Kerouac's success in conveying the notion of "IT." Dean's goal is to achieve "IT," a state of being that cannot be defined concretely, but there are frantic methods that seem helpful in reaching that metaphorical dominion where time stops and everyday concerns fall away. Dean and Sal observe "the wild, ecstatic Rollo Greb" while they are in the midst of a chaotic holiday season of parties when, as Sal observes, "everything happened" (127). Kerouac developed the mood further in *Visions of Cody* by recalling the delirious atmosphere during the Christmas season, 1948, especially since the group was discovering the bop saxophones of Dexter Gordon and Wardell Gray in a song called "The Hunt" (346). The musicians' frenzied playing typified perfectly the hunt or quest on which Sal follows Dean. Dean insists that Rollo Greb had found the secret for which they are searching. When Sal questions Dean about the nature of the secret, Dean responds cryptically, "I'll tell you—now no time, we have no time now" (127). What at first appears to be Dean's refusal to answer is in fact the perfect answer. With the clarity usually associated with Zen Buddhism, Dean has pointed directly at the answer rather than providing an insufficient response through analogy. Dean says that if they were to tune into the moment with utter attention and involvement, then of course there would be "no time." Instead, there would only be "now." He provides as clearly as possible and without development that one alternative for beat success: be here now; swing with the moment, as Greb does. Sal misses the significance of Dean's response, as he misses other important points through the story, but Kerouac as controlling author knows. Dean reaches perhaps his most acute insight when he completes the subject/object dissolution while driving high in Mexico: "this road drives *me*!" Alan Watts writes about such a state in *The Way of Zen.* He describes the goal of Zen practice to be "a total clarity and presence of mind. . . . Through such awarenesses it is seen that the separation of the thinker from the thought, the knower from the known, the subject from the object, is purely abstract. There is not mind on the one hand and its experiences on the other: there is just a process of experiencing in which there is nothing to be grasped, as an object, and no one, as a subject, to grasp it" (53).

Another time Sal again asks Dean to explain "IT" in terms of the jazz music they had heard in San Francisco. The key moment, Dean says, is when time stops and the musician draws upon the material of everyone's lives to fill the vacuum that surrounds them (206). Essentially this is the song that Kerouac learns to play too. He works with empty pages and fills them with the stories of peoples' lives that plumb their depths. His spontaneous method develops until he is extemporizing as a jazz musician does, but with words, as he says in his introduction to *Mexico City Blues* (1959). After Dean explains what he means by "IT" through jazz, he launches into a remembrance from his past, exclaiming, "NOW, I have IT" (207). Like Dexter Gordon and Wardell Gray, Sal and Dean jam together as they ride, playing off each other's ideas, coming in with new impressions, and keeping the excitement of their conversation flowing. These language breakthroughs allowed Kerouac to see the possibilities that hovered in his near future as a writer, and in *Visions of Cody,* the book he began soon after finishing *On the Road,* he strives to achieve "IT" in written prose.

CHAPTER FIVE

Visions of Cody (1972)

On the Road relates in a general way the composition of *The Town and the City*. *Visions of Cody* relates with immediacy and in detail the account of its own creation. It is also Kerouac's retelling of *On the Road*. Kerouac expressed to Cassady that when he wrote *On the Road* in 1951 he had not yet developed a deep, exploratory prose style and was instead influenced by Dashiell Hammett and William Burroughs (*Letters* 473). In short, he had matched the prose style to the picaresque subject and frenetic ambience of the book. Kerouac would change before he wrote *Visions of Cody*; he discovered a new way of writing which he called "Sketching," influenced in part by the prose of French novelist Marcel Proust (*Letters* 473). In *Visions of Cody* his subject is not exclusively the road itself and the episodic traveling on it. Rather this book focuses on Cassady himself as representative of a vanishing breed of American, the man who can swagger into a bar or prop his thumbs in his suit vest and "smile the smile of his grandfathers" (48). Kerouac seeks to match America's loss of grandeur with a suitably grandiose but lamenting and exploratory prose. In addition, this book represents Kerouac's first sustained attempt at creating an experimental novel; he had no desire to write a conventional prose account of his unconventional subject. This attempt puts Kerouac in the company of other avant-garde writers, such as James Joyce and William Faulkner, who also experimented with new expressions in language.

Kerouac did not center the book around a plot or story; yet even though no clear center exists, various definite sections are set off and strong themes persist in the otherwise loose form of the book. Kerouac is sometimes compared to Jackson Pollock, who painted in a spontaneous style in which he used the whole canvas; no area specifically draws the eye more than another, and there is no renaissance perspective. Just as Pollock involved himself with every drip of paint rather than focusing on traditional notions of background, foreground, and composition, in this book Kerouac ignores traditional novel-writing conceits. Kerouac involves himself throughout, on several occasions losing (or relinquishing deliberately) control of the narrative and even of the language itself. At these moments even his close friends advised him that the writing was not very good, but if one observes the book as a whole—the motion, energy, miasma, chaos—Kerouac successfully transmits some portion of the energy of his time, the winsomeness of his subject, and the brilliance of his insight. Furthermore, *Visions of Cody* unshrouds the mysteries of the young jailkid introduced in *On the Road,* digging into Cassady's life before and after the adventures recorded in that best-selling book.

Kerouac laments the passing of the unselfconscious, joy-loving, loud-laughing character who could look a man in the eye and slap his back, who would frequent the raucous neighborhood parties of Kerouac's youth in Lowell (264). Poet and friend Gary Snyder once remarked that Kerouac saw Cassady, aptly called "Cody" in this book, as "the last cowboy crashing." Kerouac swells his subject constantly to include his vision of America: Cody travels "across the gleaming and groaning continent of America where his fathers had all got lost" (357).

Before typing his *On the Road* scroll in the spring of 1951, Kerouac had written thousands of words about Cassady's early years in Denver, and this prose would eventually become the beginning of part 2 of *Visions of Cody.* He told Cassady that this new version contained better writing than he had produced before; the sentences were more complex, he said, and the ideas more visionary (*Letters* 327). For example, one sentence early in this section covers twenty-six lines in the published book and casts Cody's appearance on the Denver poolroom scene against a backdrop of the Pensacola Kid, Bat Masterson, Jelly Roll Morton, and the "almost metaphysical click and play of billiard balls," finally concluding with Cody's discovery of his soul (49).

More developments were soon to come. Duluoz (Kerouac's name in this book) mentions October 25, 1951, the date of his breakthrough with sketching, as "the great moment of discovering of my soul" (93). Writing to Ginsberg later, Kerouac recalled that he discovered the ability to write in a new, fresh way on October 25 when he

began sketching everything in sight, so that *On the Road* took its turn from conventional narrative survey of road trips etc. into a big multi-dimensional conscious and subconscious character invocation of Neal in his whirlwinds. Sketching (Ed White [a Columbia University schoolmate] casually mentioned it in 124th Chinese restaurant near Columbia, "Why don't you just sketch in the streets like a painter but with words") which I did. (*Letters* 356)

VISIONS OF CODY

The scenes that Kerouac sketched include the ones that begin *Visions of Cody.* Thirty brief sketches, most of them barely a page long, describe an old diner, the Capricio B-movie theater, the Third Avenue elevated subway track, and various other scenes. Cody is rarely mentioned. Yet the scenes as they appear would not have been recorded except for Cody's influence. Duluoz has learned from Cody to pay attention to details such as a sooty, decrepit music store with old newspapers and other debris blown up against the door (5). In addition, the selection of these scenes sets the tone and atmosphere for Cody's eventual arrival in the book. For example, Duluoz notes that an "oldfashioned railroad" diner is the kind Cody and his father once frequented. The Friday night beer joints in New York that Duluoz sketches have common traits with the ones Cody knows in Denver (13), and the face of an invalid on the subway may have resembled the face of a cripple who had plagued Cody as a child (19).

Kerouac's discovery of sketching in his notebooks merged with his skills as a lightning typist as he proceeded toward the technique of spontaneous prose. John Clellon Holmes observed that while typing *On the Road* Kerouac "could disassociate himself from his fingers and he was simply following the movie in his head" (Gifford and Lee 156). As the pace of composition increased, Kerouac used periods less frequently in his sketches; he now developed the dash to separate his ideas. In the following passage, dashes create a sense of overlapping aural imagery: "—happens to be a fog—distant low of a klaxon moaning horn—sudden swash of locomotive steam, either that or crash of steel rods—a car washing by with the sound we all know from city dawns—" (9). Kerouac recorded sensory impressions as he received them, transmitting them dutifully in his notebook.

Kerouac mentions October 1951 again in a letter to John Clellon Holmes. He recalls one night in particular when he was listening to live jazz and he determined at that moment to reinvigorate his writing style (*The Portable Jack Kerouac* 10). Relying on jazz terms and practice habits as metaphors for his own style, he writes in *Visions of Cody* that he is learning to write in the way that jazz musicians learn to play; he is practicing in the woodshed, metaphorically speaking, and improvising as he goes along. The song is fresh and spontaneous, and even the musician/writer is aware of mistakes that can be made (329). Kerouac's success relies on a fine balance between considering the appropriate words and actions for his book—to avoid mistakes—while at the same time knowing that time is passing by without stopping and, according to the adage, he who hesitates is lost. Kerouac must be involved totally in the moment, in the creative act, for his work to ring with the frequency of life as he perceives it; sketching techniques combined with jazz inspiration as Kerouac developed spontaneous prose.

The title *Visions of Cody* works three ways; the book consists of visions that Cody *has* or *has had* and of Duluoz's most important visions of Cody as well (295–306). Also, late in the book, Duluoz admits that he thinks Cody can read his thoughts, *"so I'll look on the world like he does"* (298). Duluoz manages a sympathetic perception and for a time sees the world as Cody must have seen it with all its beat characters, cigarette butts, and vacant lots. He has acquired Cody's vision. He concludes the first section of the book with a letter that he has written to Cody in which he admits his debt (38). Cody has shown him the value in plummeting onward and keeping the flow of language going. Duluoz tells Cody that he will accept his offer to come live with him and his wife in San Francisco, and that he will approach the house with all his senses opened up in an attempt to appreciate every detail of his arrival (42–43). Duluoz has learned the manner of capturing the moment in his writing by carrying little notebooks in which to sketch. This letter to Cody has a clear resemblance to the letter Kerouac sent Ginsberg when he announced his sketching technique discovery.

The first section of *Visions of Cody,* then, establishes the setting and tone appropriate for Cody's story and reveals the method of the writer at work. As Sal "shambled" after Dean, Duluoz shambles after Cody, but this time he is following his mentor not to physical spaces along the road; he follows him to metaphysical spaces where time slows down to allow for the keen penetration into the nature of things. That is, Duluoz has been on the road with Cody, but those adventures are in the past. One lesson that stays with Duluoz, however, is how to perceive—the vision of Cody. The prose, as poet Robert Creeley said, is "'with it,' as jazz was, not 'about it'" (*The Portable Jack Kerouac* 482). One may observe that *On the Road,* despite its inspired jazz passages, was primarily "about it," while *Visions of Cody is* it: writing is performance. In writing spontaneous prose Kerouac achieves "IT."

Kerouac acknowledges the earlier *On the Road* and his departure from it. *On the Road* finishes with these words: "I think of Dean Moriarty." Near the beginning of *Visions of Cody,* however, Duluoz notes that in the autumn of 1951 he "began thinking of Cody Pomeray, thinking of Cody Pomeray" (5) and essentially embarking on this new work. In *On the Road* Sal is confident he will find "girls, visions, everything" (11) on his road of adventure. Sal feels a pain in his heart every time he sees a beautiful girl "going the opposite direction in this too-big world" (81). The narrator in *Visions of Cody* is not so romantic: "It no longer makes me cry and die and tear myself to see her go because everything goes away from me like that now—girls, visions, anything" (33). In fact, one major theme in *Visions of Cody* is Duluoz's acceptance of loss.

The second section begins with a long examination of a single day in young Cody's life that Duluoz must have learned about from Cody's stories and letters. Duluoz records the events of the afternoon when Cody enters the pool hall and meets pool hustler Tom Watson. The protracted, sometimes interminable sentences encompass many additional details, though, including the facts of Cody's father's life and livelihood, the magazines and comics Cody read, and Cody's Gatsby-like regimen in the schedule of his days. Throughout the narrative Kerouac relies on the interior narrative he had used in *The Town and the City*. For example, when Watson asks Cody why he stares at a spot on the floor, he cannot respond (65–66). As his spokesperson, though, Kerouac had just written three hundred words revealing Cody's thoughts. Kerouac continues to defend and illuminate Cassady as he does in *On the Road*.

The day Cody meets Watson becomes the division between his anonymous youth and his new status as pool hall gang leader. Just as a kid thirsts for orange soda yet after years of experience seeks the joy of man's whiskey, Cody now seeks the excitement of downtown at night (79). Yet this joy has a boundary and is limited by the reality of the grittiness and dourness of life. Cody pursues the image of the "redbrick wall behind the neon" with both desperation and hope. For Kerouac the image is as alluring and as pathetic as the scene of Don Quixote tilting at windmills (79). Like the reflected light of *The Town and the City,* the redbrick wall behind the neon is a dominant image in *Visions of Cody.* The red neon is the titillation of Saturday night excitement, and combined with the blunt red brick behind, it represents the sordid aspects of the country, the loneliness, the senseless drinking, the evil intentions of authorities. Duluoz fears even that the law enforcement has become corrupt, and policemen are represented by their menacing patrol cars, racing from the scenes of their own nameless crimes (90).

After relaying these details of Cody's early life, Duluoz prepares to travel West to stay with Cody and his wife. Duluoz regards the galley proofs of his first novel, *H and the C* (a reference to *The Town and the City*), which he has thrown away in the trash can. He reflects that he may be "throwing away [his] life there" too, but he has made a clear break with his past. In the interest of his art, he needs to go West and see Cody and do new writing; Duluoz will salvage the waste of his recent life by creating a new universe in prose (93). Duluoz realizes that his comments represent hubris, but he does not fear the gods and will "catch thunderbolts and pull [them] down" if they try to hinder him. Having worked out the techniques of sketching and realizing its significance, and having written all he can of Cody's youthful development, Duluoz heads west to confront his hero full on and to write the story he knows is within him.

Duluoz writes minute details of his preparation and his journey, listing the belongings he will take and those he will leave. That is, he consciously chooses the effects of his past life that are worth keeping and prunes away those that are no longer valuable in the completion of this book. His text reads more like a notebook of plans than a novel: "Now what I'm going to do is this" (98). He realizes that he will need a tape recorder because, as fast as he types, he cannot keep up with the flow of events around him. He sees these tape recordings as kin to Proust's novels. They would have their own kind of logic despite the formlessness of their conception. Duluoz is announcing the form of the book itself, even though he is writing it as it develops. In this sense, at least, the book is one of the most interesting experiments in American literature. Duluoz, in his hubris, expects that he will accomplish all he projects, even though he is not sure how he will do it. The task of capturing the present moment, with all its associations and manifestations, is so difficult that Duluoz fears he will need multiple personalities, radiant intelligence, and the power of a river (99). Duluoz has set himself to the obligation and responsibility of corralling in language all that his imaginative mind perceives before him, and in this way he will write the Duluoz Legend: "I struggle in the dark with the enormity of my soul, trying desperately to be a great rememberer redeeming life from darkness" (103).

When Duluoz arrives at Cody's house, the narrative changes and the book continues instead with a transcription of a tape-recorded conversation between Jack and Cody. After 116 pages of buildup, when Duluoz finally is in Cody's pres-

VISIONS OF CODY

ence, he lets Cody do his own talking. One effect of this transcription is that after all Duluoz's recounting of the past and his
heightened artistic sense of presentation, Cody himself steps
into the book, free of Duluoz's lens. Cody speaks for himself,
present tense, without the interference of a writer, a literary go-
between. Ginsberg says in the introduction to the book that the
transcriptions are "interesting if you want the character's reality" (viii).

   The tape transcripts can be difficult to read for two reasons. First, they are transcribed, one must assume, with unerr-
ing verisimilitude. We hear the two men with all their "uhs,"
false starts, interruptions, and sudden breaks. Yet there is
another difficulty that may be even tougher for readers to sur-
mount. The characters talk in intimate terms about events that
have not been revealed to the reader. The tapes start in medias
res, in the midst of an ongoing conversation:

   JACK. —and during the night he said "I'm an artist!"
   CODY. Oh no! he he ha ha ha, he did huh? (119)

The conversation continues to involve characters the reader
does not know, in places that are not identified, doing things
that are never carried to completion, at least in the conversation. The transcripts document five nights of tape-recorded
conversations. Jack and Cody are high on marijuana and at
times painfully self-conscious of the tape recorder's presence:

   CODY. Yeah. Well I'll tell you man, the interesting thing
      about this stuff is I think the both of us are going

> around containing ourselves, you know what I mean,
> what I'm saying is, ah, we're still aware of ourselves,
> even when we're high[.]

JACK. Well I feel like an old fool[.] (128–29)

Carolyn Cassady, Neal's wife, was present for much of the taped conversations, and she recalls that she was interested in witnessing the effects of marijuana on the two men. She notes that the marijuana "was not responsible for any exceptional cleverness, only for making them think they were being clever. In fact, it seemed to me that nothing they expressed showed any really heightened perception; they were so high that dumb things just didn't sound dumb" (*Off the Road* 170).

On the second night of recording, Jack has already transcribed the first night's tapes, and the discussion about those tapes becomes the topic—another instance of Kerouac's postmodern practice of writing about writing. First the two smoke marijuana, and then the deliberation begins. They review the transcript as they involve themselves in the evening's activities of playing jazz records, and the result is a running commentary on the previous evening's conversation, a dialogue within a dialogue. By now the reader may feel that the mysteries regarding the topic are not as important to the reader as the methods of discussion are. Jack and Cody value inwardly spiraling dialogue and mutual concern over historical fact. They use the facts as a foundation, and indeed they are concerned with getting their stories told, but what seems important are the nuances of shared conversation with mutual understanding.

On the third night, Jack proves to be able to write while Cody admires the work. Of a book Jack is writing, Cody announces that Jack is writing the very prose he wishes he were capable of producing himself (151). Earlier Jack had reassured him, "You don't have to get it down" (123). As if to show Cody the ease with which books can be written, Jack proceeds to compose on the spot. Jack types a brief description of the moment: "THE TAPE RECORDER IS TURNING, THE TYPEWRITER IS WAITING" (154). Jack includes the passing moment in his prose while Cody waits for a sentence to be formalized. In a sense, Jack shows Cody's storytelling gifts but also his shortcomings as a writer, underscoring again Cody's need for Jack, the consummate writer, to tell his story.

The fourth section of *Visions of Cody* is "Imitation of the Tape," a free-flowing spiel of loosely connected language. Years later Kerouac wrote, "often I'll read me a string of talk from my head and see what it says" (*Desolation Angels* 137). One can see the results of such writing in *Old Angel Midnight* and in his long poem "Sea," included at the end of *Big Sur.* In these and similar works Kerouac sought to imitate the flow of his mind, to capture the very thoughts and the "sounds" of those thoughts as they interact with the scene around him and/or with other thoughts. A seemingly endless chain ensues, with one link always leading to another. A writer can do only so much in this direction, however, before the reader wanders lost in the language, removed from any "regular" sense that keeps reader interest. In the middle of a lengthy jazz solo, a musician may lose track of the melody and indulge in "blowing," creating free-form sound that approximates feelings and emotional textures. Before long, though, he or she returns to the recognizable strain. Kerouac writes in a free form repeatedly in his spontaneous prose, yet rarely does he stray for such an extended period as he does in the "Imitation" section. Years later he confessed, "I'd gone so far to the edges of language where the babble of the subconscious begins . . . I began to rely too much on babble in my nervous race away from cantish cliches, chased the proton too close with my microscope, ended up ravingly enslaved to sounds" ("The First Word" 190–91).

When Kerouac's most sympathetic colleague, Allen Ginsberg, read the manuscript in 1952, he was bewildered. Although he found high merit in the expository sections and the sketches, he told Kerouac that the "Imitation" section was "just a hangup" and that it contributed to the book being "crazy in a bad way." Then Ginsberg launched into a parody of the language: "an't you read what I'm shayinoo im tryinting think try I mea mama thatsshokay but you gotta make sense you gotta muk sense, jub, jack, fik, anyone can bup it, you bubblerel, Zagg" (*Letters* 373–74). Ginsberg recommended that Kerouac cut most of the "Imitation" section, a suggestion that must have made Kerouac feel no one would ever understand, let alone appreciate, what he was attempting to do. Two years later Kerouac himself wondered whether he could tread successfully the thin line between nonsense and deep meaning (*Some of the Dharma* 383).

Three years after Kerouac's death, the complete *Visions of Cody* was published, and Ginsberg was one of the first to acknowledge the quality of the writing. In the foreword to the book Ginsberg realizes that Kerouac "obviously gave up entirely on American Lit., on *Town & City,* on *On the Road,* on Himself, & his history, and let his mind loose" (*Visions of Cody* ix). Although Kerouac mentions topics that have been important in his Legend, and at times he begins to write in memoir, essay, or story modes, he catches himself and deliberately leads the prose away from narrative: "YOU'VE GOT TO MAKE UP YOUR GODDAMN MIND IF YOU WANT TO GOOF OR DON'T WANT TO GOOF OR WANT TO STAY ON ONE LEVEL KICK OR GOOF AND KICK ALONG MISSPELLING" (255). At times he moves along smoothly and can enjoy a joke at his own expense—"English almost wasn't it?" (250)—but also he realizes the inherent failure of his own experiment. Just as every high moment in *On the Road* was followed by a low point, many moments of free prose in this section are followed by Kerouac's realization of the outlandishness of his writing and the difficulty in sustaining that kind of prose. At times he treads the fine line between sense and nonsense, and despite his vow to "goof," sometimes he must make sense. He even invokes his father's printing trade business when he defines a Linotype machine as a device that can "save madness from wild scripts" (265).

Just as a jazz musician returns after a free-form jam to a recognizable melody and recovers the familiar mode of the music, one of Kerouac's most successful pieces of spontaneous prose follows the "Imitation" section. Kerouac keeps the loose phrasing and free association, but now he has a definite focus, a "jewel center," the on-location filming of a Hollywood movie. Carolyn Cassady remembers the evening that Kerouac found the shooting taking place near their Russian Hill neighborhood: "One blustery night, Jack went out alone but came back in a few minutes and tried to get Neal and me as excited as he was about having discovered that Joan Crawford was only a block away making a movie. For some reason neither Neal nor I wanted to go, and Jack went out with his notebook. Hours later he returned and stayed up all night writing 'Joan Crawford in the Fog'" (*Off the Road* 171).

The first sentence sums up one theme of the section and metaphorically describes the position Kerouac sees all the people maintaining in this piece: "Joan Rawshanks stands all alone in the fog" (275). He also surveys the entire scene of the neighborhood flooded in lights and the people, like Kerouac himself, who flock to witness the spectacle. Within the great glow of the klieg lights, the whole Hollywood machine—the director, the technicians, the crew—functions to produce the film. Finally, at the heart of the drama stands Joan Rawshanks in the actual moment of her performance. The fact that she is "faking" emotions and dramatizing a fictitious scene puts everyone's actions and intentions in doubt.

Kerouac repeatedly mentions the klieg lights, powerful carbon arc lamps used specifically for making movies. Outside the influence of the lamps the fog blows, rendering details indistinct. Within the arc of the lamps, though, the scene glows in the intense focus of hyper-reality. The individuals in the crowd generally keep their anonymity, but anyone who ventures into the light, such as the two policemen who get their pictures taken by the crew photographer, risk vulnerability to their sense of privacy. The policemen seem to be props, costumed for the part, and they react with discomfort. Onstage they are not altogether sure that they are not being made fun of.

The picture of the policemen and the film of Joan Rawshanks represent moments stopped in time. The cameraman "sucked the film out of his box and plopped it, hot with reality, instant, into his pocket" (278). The cameraman's trade is the taking of pictures just as the director's trade is the making of movies and Kerouac's is the writing of books. Each of them records a moment of time, and each of them pockets the result having extracted at least the appearance of the life from the moment. Throughout *Visions of Cody* Kerouac mentions photographs and the illusion of order and stability they create. His prose record refutes the order and seemliness of the lives the photographs project.

Kerouac draws parallels between the act of filming and the act of writing spontaneous prose. The director films the scene three times after a great amount of preparation and attention to details. Kerouac, too, writes scenes from different "angles"— he repeats throughout this section that Joan is fiddling with her keys at the door, expanding time so that he can include detailed descriptions—but he will not allow himself the luxury of the editing room where his various scenes can be spliced together. Nothing winds up on the cutting room floor. Kerouac hopes to cut through the unreality of film and portray the scene as it really is, for to him Hollywood movies rely on technique— craft—and fail to reproduce reality (284). In one brief aside Kerouac mentions that the director stops the shooting and suspends the production while he moves a twig; the implication is that one should not alter the scene as it appears (284).

After "Joan Rawshanks in the Fog," Kerouac returns to Cody as his subject. Duluoz is in Denver, alone, and feels that he has lost out on the fun-spirited side of life. Enervated, he goes to find Cody in San Francisco, and on the way he receives his directive from Heaven: "go moan for man . . . and of Cody report you well and truly" (295). Immediately the next section begins: "VISIONS OF CODY." Without further regard for background, chronology, or continuity, Duluoz recounts the times he saw Cody in his glory. Behind every word, though, lurks Cody's admonition that "Time—goes—by—*fast!!*" Therefore, Duluoz manipulates time, slowing down scenes by packing in description and parenthetical expressions. One of these visions springs from a conversation he had with Cody about the Three Stooges when suddenly Cody began "to imitate the stagger of the Stooges" (303). Kerouac is at his height as a writer in this section, fusing sound and sense as he brings the Stooges to life as embodiments of Cody's goofing attitude. The Stooge vision is the physical representation of a mental and spiritual attitude, the equivalent of Dean's beatification in *On the Road* as the "HOLY GOOF." Kerouac renders the vision with language that also staggers and goofs (304). Using bop rhythms in childlike sing-song patterns, Kerouac manages to bring the silly references back to a serious, spiritual concept—*"the god bone's connected to the bone bone"*—creating a paradoxically dark but illuminating surprise.

Kerouac continues to shift perspectives and points of view, constructing his visions of Cody as a kind of arabesque, or cubist work, with differing angles juxtaposed to render one complex but whole impression. He writes dialogue for Duluoz and Cody that appears as if it had been transcribed from tape recordings. Just as he repeated the phrase "Joan Rawshanks in the fog" to add coherence to his section about the filming, here he repeats that Cody is the brother he lost, tying together the disparate elements that make up the passage.

Finally, Kerouac suggests that Cody is dead, metaphorically, for he has quieted down and become silent, as prefigured in the opening pages of *On the Road:* his "early way" has "become so much sadder and perceptive and blank" (8). Cody has difficulty expressing himself, even finishing a single coherent thought, and he scorns Jack for thinking he has "great starlight in my eyes—I ain't nothing but a simple honest pimp" (322). The distance between the two men is the heart of the conclusion of *Visions of Cody.* In the Duluoz Legend, Cody is a hero, a champion, but now Kerouac faces the real life of his relationship with his old buddy, and he misses the friend who once stopped with him to appreciate the starlight on the rails.

In the last fifty pages of the book Kerouac recounts the events of *On the Road,* adventures that he and Cody shared before he began this book and came to his late realization that "Cody is dead." The placement of this section at the end creates a strong note of pathos and nostalgia for past times. Its placement here also reinforces Kerouac's overall structure for the book; it is not a chronological narrative, for his emphasis is on visions and the discovery of the language needed to convey them. When Kerouac visits the scenes from *On the Road,* he invests them with greater poignancy than he had in the earlier book. For example, the trip that had been such a lark—when Dean, Marylou, and Sal drove west to San Francisco—now is imbued with Cody's distance from the other two.

Cody's story draws to the end as Kerouac tires of the effort to tell it. Since he had worked for three years on his road book before blasting out the story in the spring of 1951, he has little patience to retell it one more time in his expanded book. He recycles passages from *On the Road* ("shedding with sparkler dims" and "Tonight the stars'll be out," for example), but a growing weariness and wariness in telling a linear story pervade the section. At one point he realizes that he is repeating nearly word for word a scene from *On the Road,* and he interrupts himself so that he will not retell a story he had already written once (347). In the tape transcripts, Cody says, "the second or third or fourth time you tell about it or say anything like that why it comes out different and it becomes more and more modified" (145), thus lacking the essential freshness of the original, spontaneous telling.

In the final section Kerouac succeeds in reproducing the excitement of the jazz clubs he and Cody frequent, but he is bored by the task of having to fill in the details of their lives between shows. Finally, he has Cody despair of writing as an act that can be of consequence, and Duluoz can only sigh, "Not my words" (389). In the end, Kerouac seeks to include the whole American continent and by association the entire American experience in his conclusion. He paints the course of the mighty Mississippi as he charts Lester Young's jazz roots; he summons W. C. Fields and bleak train yards. The book ends in despair-filled elegy for Duluoz's lost friend. The sun rises even as Duluoz remembers watching it set with Cody, and Duluoz bids "Adios" to the king.

The powerful sense of loss in the book is one of Kerouac's major accomplishments. He yokes the disappearing diners and neighborhood familiarity with Cody's loss of enthusiasm for life. Kerouac embraces all that the wasted past means: "I not only accept loss, I am made of loss—I am made of Cody, too" (397). He evokes the spirit of the 1920s, the world his father and Cody's father knew; he evokes also the atmosphere of the 1930s, when he and Cody were growing up. They met in the 1940s and made the decade their own. By the early 1950s Kerouac felt the loss that can only be made up through good writing. As the movie camera sucked the present scene into the film, Kerouac sucked the past into the present, where he tried to render it timeless, "redeeming life from darkness." Maybe Neal Cassady had hung up his spurs and become ensconced in "stony silences," but young Cody rages on, telling his life story and inspiring Duluoz to connect with the ineffable music and relay the songs into language.

CHAPTER SIX

Doctor Sax: Faust Part Three **(1959)**

Doctor Sax is Kerouac's most fanciful and perhaps his most well-structured book. It is also his only sustained foray into a distinct literary genre: Gothic horror. More important, in this coming-of-age story Kerouac for the first time used his newly developed spontaneous prose to recover in depth his own private past, to recount memories of his childhood and probe them for significance. Kerouac had begun writing his life story in long letters to Neal Cassady in the winter of 1950–1951, and although he had allowed himself broad stylistic latitude, he had not yet developed spontaneous prose at that time.

Peering from the midst of memories and dreams or hiding "around the corner of [Duluoz's] mind" (11), Doctor Sax initially emerges fleetingly, disappearing whenever thirteen- or fourteen-year-old Jackie Duluoz attempts to focus on him. Sax is the incarnation of the elusive "something" that darts through and hovers over *The Town and the City*. But in this book Kerouac exposes and finally deflates the mystery. Doctor Sax is a compendium of assorted magazine heroes who move in darkness and are sleek, confident, yet often baffling and enigmatic. As one who knows the secrets, Sax represents hope for Jackie Duluoz, who fears growing up. Ultimately Duluoz discovers that there is nothing to fear. Kerouac commented on the subtitle of this book: "Faust thought he was fighting evil. But there is no evil, just a butter husk of doves" (Charters, *Kerouac* 101). Images of death, darkness, mystery, and a soft brown gloom tempered by glee unify the book.

After completing *Visions of Cody* in San Francisco, Kerouac traveled to Mexico City, where he could live cheaply and enjoy freedom to work. He stayed with William Burroughs, who was there to avoid the United States authorities. Kerouac established a regimen of smoking marijuana, locking himself in the bathroom for privacy, and composing *Doctor Sax* in pencil in little notebooks. Kerouac once punned that the hallucinated style of *Doctor Sax* comes from the fact that he wrote the whole book "on pot" (Berrigan 556). The marijuana allowed Kerouac to involve himself in a world of memory and imagination, and his new spontaneous prose method gave him the vehicle to convey the swirling images as they cohered around a common theme. Kerouac had been working sporadically on his Sax material since at least 1948, when he conceived a book as a child's perspective of the American Myth (*Letters* 169). In 1949 Kerouac wrote two or more chapters. The book concerned children's happiness and innocence darkened by a flooding of the town's river (*Letters* 184–85). By this time Kerouac had already worked out the major aspects of his story and needed only the time and the method to write it. When he began to write in 1952, Kerouac told Ginsberg that he would base the book on his adolescent impressions of the Shadow, a radio show and pulp fiction hero, combined with a dream he had in 1948 (*Letters* 355). Sax combines dream, memory, myth, and fancy to re-create a boy's emotional realization of "Maturity" (*Doctor Sax* 203).

As did *On the Road* and *Visions of Cody, Doctor Sax* begins with a call to describe, a kind of holy admonition to write the story. Dream and memory are the portals to one's own adolescence. Duluoz reveals first that he dreamed of his decision to describe the very texture of the sidewalk of aptly named Moody Street in his childhood Lowell (3). In his dream Duluoz admonishes himself to "take note" of his childhood friends, and as he writes he can see his friends "now on Riverside Street in the high waving dark" (7). The important word is "now," for the writer creates his own present in the moment of composition. Kerouac again seeks to "redeem life from darkness." Whether the images are revived from dream or memory is inconsequential, since "memory and dream are mixed in this mad universe" (5).

From this dream the ghosts of Duluoz's youth stride into being. Among these ghosts is Doctor Sax, whom Duluoz saw first amidst the Catholic trappings of the dark funereal interior of the church (4). Sax had already appeared in Kerouac's prose. In *On the Road* Sal Paradise explains to a girlfriend that Doctor Sax, a mysterious figure who possesses saintly characteristics, will save the world by destroying the huge snake that threatens it. The snake may turn out to be "just a husk of doves," an image that incorporates suggestions of evil and of peace (171–72).

Before young Duluoz meets Doctor Sax, though, he himself plays the role of the mysterious shadowy figure in the guise of the Black Thief. Jackie slips sleekly through his neighborhood and steals simple objects, such as swim trunks left on a rail to dry, from his friends. Jackie imitates the heroes from his

magazines as he spies on his friends and leads them to believe
there is a phantom eccentric haunting the neighborhood. Jackie
Duluoz becomes an amalgam of the Shadow and Doctor Sax,
who is an accepted cohort of the other apparitional beings (49).
Kerouac himself had assumed a similar guise as a youth when
he became the Silver Tin Can, tossing notes in tin cans through
open windows. Kerouac's childhood friends recall that he was
a big fan of the Shadow and would emit the trademark laugh:
"Mwee-hee-hee-hee-hee" (Gifford and Lee 10). Throughout
the book Duluoz lists by title the magazines that thrilled him as
a youth: *The Shadow* (although he found the radio program dis-
appointing), *Thrilling Detective, Argosy, Phantom Detective,
Operator 5, Masked Detective, Weird Tales, Star Western, Pete
Pistol, Doc Savage,* and *Tim Tyler's Flying Luck.* Duluoz
declares that the Sax myth originated on a rainy night while he
lay in bed reading (43). These books and magazines portray a
fanciful but often dark world where adults live out childhood
fantasies. Just as Jackie likes the appearance of *Pete Pistol*
magazine covers but finds the text difficult to read (15), he
comes to realize that Doctor Sax does indeed address his childhood problems but in arcane language (197). When Doctor Sax
instructs Jackie that he must enter the world of adults, though,
Sax also reflects that Jackie's innocent childhood happiness is
coming to an end (203). Doctor Sax is Jackie's guide, conduct-
ing him from a dreamy childhood into an adolescent con-
frontation with his maturing self. The world does not really
change, but Jackie's perception of it will. Jackie's discovery of
the gritty, tangible adult sphere parallels Cody Pomeray's
vision of the redbrick wall behind the neon.

Jackie hand-prints notes on his father's printing-shop paper: "The Black Thief Has Struck" (51). He leaves the notes behind after he steals simple objects from the yards of his friends. These notes represent Duluoz's early attempts to write a mysterious figure into being. He conjures the symbolic father figure who will conduct him into maturity, ward off the attendant evil, and help render him invulnerable. However, Sax is reduced at the end of the book to a vulnerable mortal himself, incapable of saving the universe single-handedly. Thus Kerouac comments on the mortality that parents—and for Kerouac especially fathers—attain as their children grow up. Sax aids the adolescent Jackie, and once he has conducted his charge into awareness of early adulthood, he appears only occasionally, "at dusk, in autumn, when the kids jump up and down and scream—he only deals in glee now" (245). This is precisely where Kerouac first found Sax in *The Town and the City,* "with the children at dusk, when they suddenly leap up and tumble over and yell in diabolical delight, for no earthly reason, as something passes by in the dark smoky air, and the children have understood so well" (*The Town and the City* 171).

Doctor Sax consists of six sections, or books. The first, "Ghosts of the Pawtucketville Night," contains Duluoz's descriptions of his Lowell neighborhood. He even draws a map of the principal streets (42). This first section establishes the tone and method of Kerouac's presentation and also introduces the essential characters. In this book Kerouac uses the blend of narrative voices that he will rely on more and more in his future books. That is, the first-person narrator is named Jack Duluoz—Jackie as a kid. The story obviously combines biographical elements from Kerouac's life imbued with fantasy, an appropriate concoction for the tale of an imaginative youth, one that corresponds to Doctor Sax's mixture of science and magic in his potions. Confusion may result for readers: Jack Kerouac invents Jack Duluoz, who tells the tale of little Jackie. Interested readers may wish to consult the biographies to see how much of Jackie's life matches Kerouac's. The jacket notes on a recent paperback edition state that "Jack Kerouac tells the story of Jack Duluoz, a French-Canadian boy growing up, as Kerouac himself did, in the dingy factory town of Lowell Massachusetts. Dr. Sax . . . is chief among the many ghosts and demons that populate Jack's fantasy world" (New York: Grove Press, New Evergreen Edition, 1987). The inherent confusion spills even into this note. One cannot determine whether "Jack's fantasy world" refers to Kerouac or Duluoz. The problem exists in most of Kerouac's future work, as it would for any novelist who creates a first-person narrator to tell a version of his or her own past. One may simplify the matter this way: Duluoz conducts readers through Kerouac's artistically intensified past.

As Duluoz reconstructs the scenes of his youth, he battles the forces of decay. From his present perspective, Duluoz knows that childhood pal Dickey Hampshire died in World War II, a neighborhood school has since burned down, and the high school fence is "fast losing posts to space and time" (52). Even Jackie's marble racehorses grew fast and then grew old, just as real racehorses do (101). Kerouac again recapitulates the theme of loss and collapse that he explored in his first three books; in this instance he draws on the metaphor of a house collapsing from within (77). As a writer, Duluoz can freeze time and restore the scenes of his youth by summoning them up in memory and preserving them in prose. Jackie Duluoz can create his own time, too, as he invents his own clock with a Victrola turntable motor and uses it to time his friends in track events. While G. J. runs the "Five Lap 'Mile,'" Duluoz's imagination roams the Lowell summer evening, noting the stars and shadows, so that when G. J. completes the mile, his time seemed "miserably slow" (55). Kerouac had discovered the method of manipulating time while writing *Visions of Cody* as he repeated scenes from different angles or interjected long asides in the middle of an action or a piece of dialogue. Duluoz freezes many moments in *Doctor Sax*. In one instance, Jackie's friend Scotty Boldieu pitches a baseball game. After he winds up but before he delivers the pitch, Scotty observes the beauty of the sky as well as the surrounding neighborhood and even various principal points of interest before he kicks and fires his pitch to the catcher (*Doctor Sax* 38).

The twenty-five separate scenes of "A Gloomy Book-movie" make up book 2 of *Doctor Sax*. Kerouac writes in present tense, so each scene is further removed from the passage of time. No time passes; all time is now. The "bookmovie" portrays three distinct memories: the afternoon of a great thunderstorm, Duluoz's make-believe horse-race game he played with marbles, and a night at the Pawtucketville Social Club when a Sax-like character plays pool. The first memory demonstrates Duluoz's awe with natural events—which sets up the later flood scene and the night of the great snake. The second memory relates his ability to imagine whole realities—which sets up

DOCTOR SAX

his writing of this book from fantasy. And the third reveals his perception of Sax as part of the adult world—the theme of this book. These scenes also represent Kerouac's continuing experimentation with language and novel form. Rather than the conventional division of paragraphs, Kerouac uses sudden scene changes, as in a movie, to divide his thematic units. Some scenes consist of only one sentence or even one phrase, flashing rapidly across the mental movie screen. Many of the scenes direct the reader to picture a specific location and cinematically combine sound and sight (82–85).

In book 4 Doctor Sax, "no sophisticated writer," has produced a manuscript (135). The story concerns a party at the castle attended by pretentious artists and self-important acting students. The party goes on until a young woman spies Doctor Sax peering in a window and screams. Sax invades the party and horrifies everyone with his self-described purple face, red hair, and red eyebrows. He leaves with his evil laughter echoing in the halls. In addition to expanding the characterization of Doctor Sax, the story serves also to contrast Kerouac's writing style with Sax's traditional narrative. The two are working essentially the same material, but the differences clearly indicate who is "no sophisticated writer" and who is manipulating language and narrative form to dramatic effect.

Book 3, "More Ghosts," is the shortest section. Kerouac resurrects his favorite image of the redbrick wall behind the red neon lights, appropriately set in the neighborhood of a movie theater and a candy store (110). The entire fourth chapter of book 3 describes the alley that runs along these two buildings. Lowell's mystery lies somewhere in the image of this alley; "it lurks in the shadows of the redbrick walls" (113). Yet the red softness is blanketed by "some kind of brown tragedy . . . brown gloom of midnight cities presses the windows in" (112). Kerouac's color imagery paints the fundamental sources of his adolescent yearning and disillusionment. He associates brown with home and his mother but also with anguish. One key image in the book is Duluoz's "Great Bathrobe Vision." At the age of three years or less, Jackie lay in his mother's arms wrapped in her brown bathrobe, and from that moment the color brown became the dominant hue of his family life for its warmth but also for its resonance of gloom (18). Later he recalls the brown gloominess in the nooks of his house (82). In adolescence, Saturday night excitement grows for Jackie Duluoz, but it is tempered by the pervasive melancholy of the mature Duluoz's memories. The redbrick alley walls bring an abrupt end to the titillation of the red neon, and the pervasive brown gloom wraps Duluoz's life in the warm and homey yet enervating blanket of his family. Doctor Sax's color is black, the color of deep, impenetrable mystery, the imitation of which Jackie sought when he became the Black Thief. Doctor Sax admonishes Jackie to perceive his life as an existence shrouded in darkness (76), yet the bright sunny October mornings have taught Jackie that "*all my life wasn't black*" (38). When the great snake finally appears, some castle characters predict that "clouds of Seminal Gray Doves shall issue forth from the snake's mouth" (109), symbolizing Jackie's ripening sexuality.

Just after Kerouac turned fourteen in March 1936, the Merrimack River flooded Lowell. In book 5, "The Flood," Duluoz focuses on the symbolic aspects of the flood, which, as

Doctor Sax would soon reveal, brings the situation to a climax (194). Although Jackie and his friends, like typical adolescents, are quite excited about the flood, the event bears enormous importance in Jackie's life. As the floodwaters roar down the Merrimack, Duluoz stands on the precarious edge of the river (162); he was poised on the brink between his childhood and his impending manhood. The sandbanks along the river had been their playgrounds, but now the serious implications of the flood transform the scene from childhood playgrounds to adult seriousness and danger (166).

Book 5 ends on Friday as the river begins to recede, and book 6, "The Castle," portrays the events of the next day. Jackie finally meets Doctor Sax, the mysterious figure who has been haunting him all these days and nights. When Doctor Sax reveals the intimate knowledge he has of Jackie's private life, Jackie recognizes Doctor Sax as his friend, not an evil phantom. The two glide from shadow to shadow together while Sax comments on the malignant night that awaits them. Cryptically, Doctor Sax tells Jackie of his impending future: civilization, sex, solitude, nightmares, love, old age, and death. Jackie must leave behind the world of adventure magazines for the real world of adults, even though this means leaving behind also the innocent happiness he has known. Jackie and Doctor Sax visit scenes of Jackie's family, who move about unaware of the great dangers. Jackie realizes the enormity of the snake, the horror of its imminent arrival, and stammers that he only wished to look at the river; he was not prepared for an apocalypse (236). Nonetheless, there is nowhere for him to escape, since the whole world is involved. In its first rumbling tremors, the snake destroys the castle and its inhabitants except for Doc-tor Sax. Sax loses all his power though; his slouch hat and cape are cast off and he becomes just a regular guy in the clothing of a blue-collar workman. He possesses neither mystique nor magic (240). His herb potions were worthless. Just as Cody lost his powers at the end of *Visions of Cody,* Sax too has become just an ordinary person. Kerouac borrows an image from the Mexican flag, and a great black bird descends from the sky and takes the snake off in its beak. Doctor Sax is amazed even as he is chagrined at his own powerlessness and uselessness: "The Universe disposes of its own evil" (245). Jackie is now Jack, and he sees the world for what it is. The great threat had not been a cosmic imbalance after all; the universe does not need people's interference for its mechanisms to continue. The snake is gone; Doctor Sax diminishes as the flood ebbs. Jack passes the Grotto, a small park dedicated to Catholic prayer which been haunted earlier by Doctor Sax. This time Jack sees just the crucifix on a mound of earth where old women pray in reverence (245). Breaking from the imagery of shrouds, dark altars, and slouch hats, Jack puts a flower in his hair, an emblem of his deliverance from the black world of Doctor Sax.

CHAPTER SEVEN

Maggie Cassidy (1959) and *The Subterraneans* (1958)

Kerouac wrote two "true-story novels" in 1953, *Maggie Cassidy* beginning in January and *The Subterraneans* in three nights in October. The first book deals with his first love, a high school romance with a Lowell girl, Mary Carney. The second book concerns his affair with a black woman in New York City, Alene Lee, named Mardou Fox in the book. Taken together, the books represent again Kerouac's split between the town and the city. In *Maggie Cassidy* Kerouac looks to an increasingly distant past and his romanticized high school days. *The Subterraneans,* on the other hand, records events recent to the time of composition. Kerouac wrote the first half of *Tristessa,* the tale of his love for a Mexican junky, in the summer of 1955, the next true story-novel he wrote after *The Subterraneans.* That is, he wrote three consecutive books about his love affairs with women, and each plays off ideas and tensions from the others. *Tristessa* marks the entrance of Buddhism into Kerouac's prose, so that book is included in the next chapter.

Though Kerouac titles two of the books after their woman characters, the central character in each book is Kerouac's alter ego: Leo Percepied in *The Subterraneans* and Jack Duluoz in the other two. The books begin and end with the narrator's solitude, and the narrator rarely enters the minds of the female characters sufficiently to convey their thoughts and motivations to the reader.[1] In each case the narrator's incapacity for understanding the women characters determines his fate as an outsider, destined to write about the world in which he yearns to belong. In each case, too, the reader can see the women as "native." That is, Maggie embodies Lowell with her Irish background, working-class roots, and "local girl's attitudes"; Mardou is innately of the Village,[2] where she knows all the jargon and moves in the hip circles; Tristessa, more than the others, is the "fellaheen" companion Sal Paradise searches for in *On the Road* and believes he had found in Terry, the Mexican woman. The narrator sees each as having that sense of place for which he himself has searched. As does Neal Cassady, "a western kinsman of the sun," these women represent an aboriginal, natural presence, and with this genuineness comes a kind of dignity, a regal sense of being themselves. Compelled to devote his life to writing, the narrator exchanges the possibility of an enduring love life for the necessity of art. As did Sal Paradise in *On the Road,* the narrator in these stories—especially in *The Subterraneans* and *Tristessa*— stores up experiences expressly for writing them later. This is not to say that the experiences were shallow because the narrator saw their potential for use in books. The narrator is painfully aware of the trade-off he makes. As with all of Kerouac's books, the essential story is the language itself and Kerouac's manipulation of language to mirror and intensify reality. Kerouac had developed his spontaneous prose techniques fully and was experienced in using them by the time he wrote these works.

Maggie Cassidy

In writing *Maggie Cassidy* Kerouac used many of the same characters from *Doctor Sax:* G. J., Scotty Boldieu, and others reappear, and this time "Jackie" of *Doctor Sax* is "Jacky" Duluoz, though his friends often call him "Zagg," Kerouac's own nickname acquired during his teenage years. Maggie would soon call him by his mature name, "Jack." The story begins three years after the *Sax* episodes, on New Year's Eve 1939, the last holiday season untainted by the ominous war in Europe that would scatter the high school friends and bring a somber note to their revelries. As the five boys walk along the snowy sidewalk on their way to a dance, G. J. sings "*Jack o diamonds, Jack o Diamonds, you'll be my downfall,*" but the narrator notes that G. J. knows only part of the lyrics. The fact that he does not know "the downfall part of it" (7) helps preserve the light mood of the beginning of the book while hinting that the boys' ignorance permits this bliss. The world war that hovers darkly is not yet under way, the song lyrics are without ruin and undoing, and Jacky has not yet fallen in love with Maggie, a relationship that will end with Jack "sick, cursing" (189).

The opening narrative represents Kerouac's only use of third-person narration after *The Town and the City.* The third-person narrator sets the scene and reveals only Duluoz's thoughts. Duluoz's friends call him "Memory Babe" and know him to be a word-slinger (12). Yet in the first four sections of the book, the pensive Duluoz rarely speaks since the others are so boisterous. They pass other boys who are off on dates with young women. The recently "matured" Billy Artaud has a steady girlfriend, and even the hulking, simple Iddyboy has a date with a young woman. The stage is set for Duluoz, the dreamy, inward wordsmith who is on his way to a dance, to meet the young woman who will serve as the catalyst for this book.

In section 5 the narration shifts to the first person, and Duluoz takes over the story. Instantly the older, wiser Duluoz interjects a grave and ardent statement: first he recognizes an innate relationship between love and death, and for Duluoz, "the only love can be the first love, the only death the last, the only life within, and the only word . . . choked forever" (27). Kerouac presents again his combination of bleak reality and his sense of pervasive mystery in the universe. Like Peter in *The Town and the City,* Kerouac believes there is more to life than the surface, than inevitable decay and death. Kerouac's innate sense of mystery leads him to conclude that there is a word, "the only word," but a career of writing may not be enough to utter it. Zagg can easily apply words he has gleaned from the encyclopedia, but pronouncing truth requires more than an extensive vocabulary. Awareness of this difficulty drives Kerouac to write, even as he knew of—but could not articulate—the "something" that hovers over the scenes of *The Town and the City* or "the only word" that eludes him in all his books.

Kerouac may have named Maggie Cassidy for Carolyn Cassady, with whom he was in love at the time he wrote this book. Interested readers should consult Carolyn Cassady's biography for the details of this unusual affair.[3] Duluoz romanticizes that her name must have once been "Casa d'Oro," which means "house of gold" and connotes the emotionally rich house Kerouac always pictured as home. Maggie knows he is a football player, and she asks him if he gets hurt often. One theme in *Maggie Cassidy* is that love introduces emotional pain. Duluoz hints at the sources of this coming pain and foreshadows the differences between the two young lovers. First, though Maggie is only a year older than Duluoz, the difference in their ages represents a difference in maturity too. Second, Duluoz imagines that when he is with Maggie, people see him as a child who is nearly man-sized; nonetheless, he is suspicious of "things non-Canuck, non-half-Indian" (31), a reference to his ethnic identity. Even in their first moments he senses his position as an outsider.

After the in medias res beginning of the book, Duluoz paints in section 6 the geographic background of their romance. In effect, the book starts again, and this time the scene reflects the opening of *The Town and the City,* complete with the starlight shining on the river and a lingering trace of the earlier book's style: "Still, and soft, the stars on the river run" (32). Now, however, the words frequently bang into each other rather than gliding together like the various instruments in an orchestra:

> And at night the river flows, it bears pale stars on the holy water, some sink like veils, some show like fish, the great moon that once was rose now high like a blazing milk flails its white reflection vertical and deep in the dark surgey mass wall river's grinding bed push. As in sad dream, under the streetlamp, by pocky unpaved holes in dirt, the father James Cassidy comes home with lunchpail and lantern, limping, redfaced, and turns in for supper and sleep. (33)

This paragraph represents major devices Kerouac uses throughout the book. Alliterations ("lunchpail and lantern, limping") and assonance ("as in a sad dream, under the streetlamp") increase the poetic tone of the prose. In fact, if the sentences are broken as follows, a reader might presume this is a poem:

And at night the river flows
it bears pale stars on the holy water
some sink like veils, some show like fish,
the great moon that once was rose
now high like a blazing milk flails

The recurrent iambic rhythm, the metaphors, and the compressed language bring out the poetic quality of the passage. Strong imagery, too, adds to the lyrical quality. For example, probably no two readers interpret "dark surgey mass wall river's grinding bed push" the same way, yet the phrase transmits the power of the river as it interacts with the shore. Anyone who has stood along the banks of a powerful river and marveled at its unceasing surge might understand exactly what the phrase means without requiring regular semantic sense. Kerouac refers repeatedly to the stars gleaming on the river. This image, carried over from *The Town and the City,* represents the lost carefree nights of youth, the timeless moments when children played excitedly by moonlight, when mystery and romance first crept into their minds. The river also represents the vicissitudes of time. Just as Jackie Duluoz's marble racehorses eventually crack and the high school fence posts are lost to time, the river robs him of youth even as it represents the mystery of youth. Although the river gleams in starlight, the river is also dark, murmurous, and sneaky, threatening the solidity of the shore (33–34). Symbolically, rivers represent the passage of time; Kerouac's rivers reflect the starry promise of romance, fickle as it is merely a reflection, and the ravages of time as the river's "grinding bed push" consumes the banks. Kerouac's prose, like Robert Frost's poems, can be a momentary stay against confusion. In the act of writing he again seeks to redeem life from darkness.

The closing image of the paragraph above portrays Maggie's father coming home. The lunchpail and lantern are the combination of home and work that Duluoz yearns for but will not have. Section 6 closes with the image of a freight train crossing the bridge over the river, throwing a flare of light on the children below, just as Kerouac's prose briefly illuminates the scene in this section. He gives readers a brief but bright glimpse of the scene; then, like the train, he knows his love will disappear into the night, lost down a gloomy path (34).

The story itself is not unlike many other boy-meets-girl, boy-loses-girl tales. Jealousy and the straining of young love smolder in the midst of high school scenes: notes passed in class, meetings under the big clock, track meets in which Duluoz is the star. Ultimately, New York City draws Duluoz powerfully. He invites Maggie to his prep school prom, hoping to impress her with his new sophistication. Maggie becomes jealous of his attraction to the city (179). She completes the binary opposition Kerouac explores in *The Town and the City* when she calls him "Lowell Jack Duluoz" (180).

For the final two scenes of the book, Kerouac reverts to the third-person narrator that began the novel. Three years have passed, and the reader sees Duluoz parking cars in a city garage and drinking beer. Intoxicated, he calls Maggie, and she agrees to see him. Duluoz's romanticism has waned drastically:

"'Okay baby,' said J. D. 'see ya'" (185). As he drives to their rendezvous, he links himself to the tragic subject of the song that opened the book, for he now sings "*Jack o diamonds* [an oblique reference to J. D., Jack Duluoz]*, you'll be my downfall.*" He knows all the words. He talks to himself as he drives and reveals the great differences between the Jack Maggie once knew and the person he has become; he boasts of his worldliness, including his sexual experiences, and claims "the stories I could tell you'd make your little Massachusetts Street sit pale with *this* star" (186). His last phrase parodies the romantic language of their earlier relationship, especially the river passage quoted above. Maggie instantly sees the difference in him; she says that he has become "cold hearted" (188). Drunk, he tries to force her to make love to him in the back seat of the car he has illicitly borrowed, but she refuses. Duluoz has left Lowell and his idealistic notions of the possibilities of youthful romance. He has traded his track star hero and local good-boy status for the world of gritty, beat reality, parking cars in a garage and drinking beer. Now alone, he is very different from the brakeman father who comes home at the end of the day with his lunchpail and lantern.

The Subterraneans

Less than half a year after finishing *Maggie Cassidy,* Kerouac met Alene Lee, the woman who inspired *The Subterraneans.* They had a brief affair in August 1953 that lingered into the fall. In three nights in October, high on Benzedrine, Kerouac wrote the entire novel. The first line of *The Subterraneans* parodies the traditional "Once upon a time" beginning of fairy tales: "Once I was young and had so much more orientation and could talk with nervous intelligence" (1). The tone of the book sounds like the book Duluoz began while recording taped conversations in *Visions of Cody* (151–54). In that conversation Jack remarks, "I think like this all the time but I never write this," and he later decides that the tone is like the beginning of Dostoevsky's *Notes From the Underground.* The narrator in *The Subterraneans,* whose title suggests Dostoevsky's book, also indicates that he is talking—perhaps in his head—rather than writing. The prose in this book conveys the events and the reflections on those events as they happen. Kerouac uses the bohemian hipsters and the Greenwich Village atmosphere they inhabit as the background for his story. To maintain the anonymity of his characters—especially of Alene Lee, who did not wish to be identified—Kerouac switched the setting to San Francisco. A few telltale bits of evidence remain, however. For example, in one scene several characters steal a vendor's pushcart; San Francisco had no pushcart vendors. At its root, this is simply another boy-meets-girl, boy-loses-girl tale, but instead of 1930s Lowell for his setting, the scene shifts to the world for which Duluoz left Lowell.

The book works in three primary ways. First, the troubled romance of the story itself interests readers through plot and outcome. The openly sexual romance concerns a white man and a black woman, which may intensify this interest. Kerouac wrote this book a year before the Supreme Court voted to segregate schools, ten years before the Civil Rights Act. Leo Percepied, the narrator, knows that his relationship with Mardou, based on Lee, would alienate him from his family. Warren French finds Kerouac's treatment of the sexual and racial themes in this book "a nasty bit of business indeed," for he sees this book as "a glaring example for antiracist and feminist critics of the attitudes they decry in American culture and its mainstream literary tradition. Far more than television's famous Archie Bunker, Leo Percepied is the fictional embodiment of the woman-degrading, male chauvinist, racist, and homophobic attitudes that have engendered some of the ugliest controversies in the United States since World War II" (47). Some readers may agree with French, although some others may interpret the same scenes as indications not of Percepied's narrow-minded bigotry, but instead as symptoms of his own self-admitted discomfort and lack of confidence. Having hazarded onto the social ground that he explores, Percepied may have found himself—as a white male in the mid 1950s—a venturer in unfamiliar territory. Readers may also note that every step along the way, Percepied acknowledges some mistake or other that he blunders into, and that finally he blames himself for the collapse of the relationship. Still, one would have to grant quite a bit of artistic license to allow Percepied, and by complicity Kerouac, complete freedom from French's charges.[4]

Second, the novel exposes the inner lives of urban bohemia and reveals details of the lifestyle and philosophy to which mainstream readers otherwise would not be privy. The book, like Stephen Crane's *Maggie, A Girl of the Streets* sixty years before, lets readers peer into areas that had been socially off-limits for examination. More than *On the Road,* which places beat characters in generally familiar American scenes, *The Subterraneans* takes readers directly into the neighborhoods that many people

had only read about in the tabloids. *The Subterraneans* is probably more responsible than any other Kerouac work for inspiring
such copycat paperback originals as *Beatnik Party* ("The truth
about the wild orgies of San Francisco's beat generation!"), *Sin
Hipster* ("the streets and alleys where wine, pot and lust flow like
water and a beard is your ticket to a torrent of passion"), and *Lust
Pad.* Although these copycat paperbacks are typically tongue-in-
cheek publications, their success provides evidence of America's
curiosity of the underground scene, and one can assume that
many readers took them as testimony of the actual phenomena.
The Subterraneans is the only Kerouac book made into a motion
picture, and the picture was produced during the height of the
beatnik craze. In Hollywood's watered-down version, George
Peppard stars with Leslie Caron instead of a black woman.

The book also succeeds with its language. In his first writings in which he used spontaneous prose, Kerouac's view generally was broad. *Visions of Cody,* while influenced in all areas by
Cody, deals with much more than its central figure and covers a
relatively long period. *Doctor Sax* and *Maggie Cassidy,* too,
focus on their respective themes, yet they cover long periods and
allow much leeway in the material that the narrator can include
in the basic narrative. *The Subterraneans,* on the other hand, con-
centrates exclusively on the story at hand. This close examination results in part from the fact that Kerouac wrote the whole
book in three nights quite soon after the events the book
describes.

Kerouac battled with Grove Press to have his book published as he wrote it—that is, with as little editorial interference
as possible. *Visions of Cody* was not published until after Ker-

ouac's death, and neither *Maggie Cassidy* nor *Doctor Sax* was published until 1959; thus *The Subterraneans* was his first spontaneous prose book published. He had to fight with the strength of his artistic convictions when he had very little going for him as a professional author. He wrote to his Grove editor, Donald Allen, in the spring of 1957: "I can't possibly go on as a responsible prose artist . . . if I let editors take my sentences, which are my phrases that I separate by dashes when 'I draw a breath,' . . . & riddle them with commas, cut them in half, in threes, in fours, ruining the swing, making what was reasonably wordy prose even more wordy and unnaturally awkward (because castrated)."[5] Kerouac told Allen that the preservation of his "modern language" was more important to him than the money he would earn by having his edited prose published. When Grove finally set Kerouac's book in galley proofs, Kerouac spent "five exhausting nights"—longer than it took him to write the book—restoring the prose to what he felt was its original swing. He told Allen that if there would be costs for resetting the galleys, he would gladly pay them for he believed that publication of this book would open the door to publication of his other spontaneous prose works.

Leo's constant returning to his mother and to his work separates him from Mardou, and a core theme in this book resides in Leo's indecision over whether he would rather love Mardou and commit himself to her, or whether he would rather write about the affair. Mardou is aware of Leo's split loyalty: she claims that women are the "essence" of men's desire, yet men persist in activities such as writing books that lead them away from that essence (16). Leo confesses to his readers that "the thighs contain the essence" (17) and later thinks that the essence is Mardou's womb, the goal of his desire and the source of life (110). Yet in a moment of doubt, Leo has a powerful epiphany: "I GOT MY OWN LITTLE BANGTAIL ESSENCE AND THAT ESSENCE IS MIND RECOGNITION" (48). Leo is split between discovering essence in a woman and discovering essence in his own mind, and for him the one precludes the other. Ultimately, of course, Leo chooses art, for otherwise no book would exist. As in *Maggie Cassidy,* dejection results in art, and the lost love at least yields a moment of salvation in the creation of the book.

One big difference from *Maggie Cassidy,* though, is that no filtering lens or romantic haze soothes the pains of lost love. Kerouac is so close to the events that he has difficulty beginning the book. The stammering, backtracking approach reveals a narrator who is, as he admits, unselfconfident (1). First, Leo reveals the history of the subterraneans, a name given by Adam Moorad (based on Allen Ginsberg) to a group of intelligent, literary bohemians who smoke pot and often shoot heroine and yet are somehow "Christlike." As Leo describes the subterraneans, though, he usually details the differences between them and himself. Leo helps organize pot parties and frequents the subterraneans' jazz joints so that he can "dig them as a group" (4), but his dissociation from them is clear. When his drunken escapades are at their most obnoxious, Leo dutifully records the subterraneans' reactions. One character complains that Percepied is overbearing, and he despises his presence at the party (100). The group both fascinates and repulses Leo as he observes them. Repeatedly Leo mentions that they are angels, Christlike, a new generation, while he looks like a "bum" or a "hoodlum" who once engaged in "nannybeating." His saintliness is not apparent, since he is "hot" and they are "cool." At heart, he remains a romantic with old-fashioned notions. His drunkenness, his pursuit of kicks, and his devotion to home and his mother prevent him from being a subterranean himself. Leo recently left a job on a ship because of his inability to be "like an ordinary guy" (2), and now he enters another scene where he does not belong. Kerouac continues the theme of the outsider in his Duluoz Legend. Despite its title, this book focuses on Mardou's influence by the subterraneans rather than on the subterraneans themselves. Few readers would see Leo's view of them as celebratory or even condoning.

Initially, Mardou's sensuality attracts Leo. The name Kerouac gives her, "Fox," implies both that she is foxy—that is, attractive—and that the men (hunters) pursue her for sport. Leo assumes that, like him, his male readers are also crudely sexual (3) and would therefore share his eagerness to have sex with Mardou. In fact, after a party the first night one of the "Christlike" subterraneans tells Leo, that they deserve sexual favors from their female guests since they paid for the beer and the marijuana (10). As their relationship develops, Leo sees her differently from the way the subterraneans do. Ultimately, Leo is drawn to her vulnerability and her honesty.

For Leo, Mardou embodies a long Native American descent (Leo imagines that Mardou is part Cherokee), and his association with her brings him closer to the land and its native people. In this regard, Mardou is a hipper version of Terry from *On the Road.* Leo contrasts Mardou's nobility with the subterraneans' decadence when he envisions the great civilizations of

Mardou's spiritual ancestors, The Incas, the Mayans—"as noble as Greek, Egypt"—who built glittering cities and were artistic geniuses. Then the conquerors come blundering in, caricatured as effeminate Spanish explorers (25). Mardou is a mixture of the ancient high civilizations and the emergent new one, the one populated by bop children.

As Cody had done, Mardou tells Leo her story in great detail. Her narrative makes up the next large section of the book. Leo quotes Mardou liberally, and then he breaks in with his own often lengthy analyses of her story set off by dashes or parentheses. Mardou's perceptions of her setting and her situation begin to match Cody's. Leo, like Jack Duluoz sketching in *Visions of Cody,* envisions a gleaming restaurant scene with alluring food displayed behind the window (28). The list of food items provides the proper connotative backdrop—Mardou cannot enjoy the fruits with which civilization tantalizes her.

Mardou's visions also parallel Cody's. She tells of how she "flipped" one night while hanging out with the subterraneans and of the paranoiac perceptions that resulted. She develops a powerful awareness that "everything is happening to everyone all the time everywhere," a feeling that also matches Peter Martin's in *The Town and the City.* Like Peter and Cody, Mardou feels an obligation to share the knowledge that there is no need for worry, that everything is all right. Like Cody, Mardou realizes people could live their whole lives sustained by clarity of vision and a mutual insistence to coexist in a beneficial way (34), a simplified Taoist understanding. Finally, Leo asks pithy questions that encourage Mardou to continue her narrative, just as Duluoz does for Cody in "The

Tape" section. If Kerouac's memory is as sharp as his friends reported it to be, then this section may be quite like the tape transcriptions of *Cody,* conveying the exact words, hesitations, pauses, and phrasings of Alene Lee's speech. Leo then draws the most direct comparison with Cody. Mardou's tale and her honesty and depth in telling it remind Leo of the close male friends of his youth with whom he had shared adventures and, in beatific awareness, had watched the sun rise on "symbols in the saturated gutter" (36). With this book and in this passage in particular, Kerouac ushers women into the male-dominated Beat Generation.

One motif in this book is Leo's preoccupation with homosexuality. Kerouac had not addressed the topic directly in any previous book. He eliminated the homosexual relationships from *On the Road* that had occurred between some of the men on whom he based characters. Cody speaks of his relationships with Irwin (based on Allen Ginsberg) in *Visions of Cody,* but Jack rarely confronts the implications. After witnessing Cody having homosexual sex ("Olympian perversities"), Jack is disgusted (358–59). *The Subterraneans* is full of scenes that involve homosexuality (no one used the term *gay* in 1953). Usually Leo initiates the encounters. In one instance Leo blends the genders as he observes people exiting a bar: "a beautiful thin birl or girl in boy slacks with stars in her eyes" (5). This apparent typographical error is a key to Leo's thinking as he sees both boy and girl qualities combined. His first "foolish mistake" with Mardou happens when he refuses to go home with her, preferring instead to stay at an acquaintance's apartment and look at homosexual photographs (38). One of the subterraneans accuses Leo of being "a fag" (49). On one drunken evening Leo winds up in a hotel room with Arial Lavalina (based on Gore Vidal), a well-known writer and blatant homosexual (53). Leo's submergence into the subterraneans' realm involves him in sexual ambiguity. His fixation with homosexuals comes between him and Mardou as he unconsciously looks for reasons to lose her love. He counters his and Mardou's own "forbidden" relationship—he never considers marrying her—with another forbidden sexual direction. In any case, considering the marijuana, the heavy drinking, the miscegenation, and his obsession with homosexuals, Leo is deeply involved in cultural experimentation and pushing limits.

When Leo is away from his mother, he involves himself fully in the nightlife of the city—drugs, drink, sex—with the realization that he can return home for emotional and moral cleansing. He never refers to a healthy love relationship in his past, or in anyone else's for that matter. Once he refers to being in love when he was sixteen years old, an oblique reference to *Maggie Cassidy,* but the experience only served to make him jaded. The only woman with whom he has a solid relationship is his mother. Gerald Nicosia points out that the name Leo Percepied has symbolic significance. Leo was Kerouac's father's name, and Percepied "is French for 'pierced foot.' Oedipus of Greek legend had his feet pierced as a child and derived his name indirectly from that fact, 'Oedipus' being Greek for 'swollen foot,' the condition caused by his injury" (Nicosia 449). Leo's mother is a major figure in this book, although she is always offstage. Leo reveres his mother and has taken his dead father's place in her affections. His mother represents an intimate, warm security, and in another sense his mother represents a stable environment in which to write. In the subterraneans' orbit writing is impossible, although this is where Leo explores his topic.

Kerouac's exploration of limits goes beyond social behavior, for he also explores the limits of language. One has difficulty speaking of "sentences" in this book, for his structures range far beyond the traditional sentence. Ideas flow one into the next without conventional punctuation. In fact, the ideas are usually connected by a common thread, yet Leo changes directions frequently and adds insights on top of insights until the initial point of the sentence may be lost. Leo cries out at one point, "*I'm* the bop writer" (98), insisting that the bop scene is his material but also that he writes the way a bop musician plays. His ideas are just the starting point for extemporization and openness to new ideas that come along during his "solo." In 1951 Kerouac had a daydream in which he became a master tenor sax player, capable of playing different melodies simultaneously and in different keys. This imagined musicianship parallels Kerouac's notion of the complex overlay of ideas he hoped to produce in writing.[6] Excerpts hardly show the complexity of his ideas, but a sample may suffice to help readers glimpse his method. In the following passage—excerpted from the middle of a longer section—Leo describes Easter morning as Mardou wanders in the streets after her night of "flipping":

the flowers on the corner in baskets and the old Italian in his apron with the newspapers kneeling to water, and the Chinese father in tight ecstatic suit wheeling the basketcarriaged baby down Powell with his pink-spot-cheeked wife of glitter brown eyes in her new bonnet rippling to flap in sun, there stands Mardou smiling intensely and strangely and the old eccentric lady not any more conscious of her Nergoness than the kind cripple of the store and because of her out and open face now, the clear indication of a troubled pure innocent spirit just risen from a pit in pockmarked earth and by own broken hands self-pulled to safety and salvation, the two women Mardou and the old lady in the incredibly sad empty streets of Sunday after the excitements of Saturday night. (31)

Kerouac contrasts the complex and drug-induced paranoias of the subterranean world with the simple pleasures of normal people on a Sunday morning. The rain has ended, and the sun makes the world "glitter." Mardou's night has been long, dark, and harrowing, but she now moves through a rain-cleansed morning, with the bright sunshine a symbol of the return of normalcy. Furthermore, Mardou has risen from the depths of her psychosis like Jesus from his tomb, symbolized both by Easter morning and the direct reference to the "spirit just risen from a pit." With no certain faith in a greater being, though, Mardou has had to salvage herself.

Kerouac has opened up the prose possibilities in this book, as in his previous ones, to include both a basic narrative and series of asides that comment on and expand that narrative. While he continues to develop his favorite images of Saturday night excitement versus Sunday sadness and the "lostpurity" of something as clean and free as clouds, he also finds variation on his basic techniques of spontaneous prose. No conscientious reader would mistake a passage from this book with a passage from *Maggie Cassidy*. Although both books represent Kerouac's spontaneous prose at its finest, the tone and intensity are distinct for each book.

CHAPTER EIGHT

Tristessa (1960), *Visions of Gerard* (1963), and Buddhism

Although linked to *Maggie Cassidy* and *The Subterraneans,* *Tristessa* represents a departure in Kerouac's true-story novels. An important distinction between this book and the previous true-story novels Kerouac had written concerns his discovery of Buddhism in the late winter of 1953 and spring of 1954. One cannot overstate the significance of Kerouac's Buddhist studies on his life and his writing. At its core, Kerouac's Buddhism was not a radical departure from his worldview, for he had been exploring key Buddhist issues since *The Town and the City* without the background of Buddhism's rich traditions. He found affirmation in Buddhist teachings that made sense in the universe as he knew it. Kerouac augmented rather than replaced his childhood religious beliefs. According to Ann Charters, "Kerouac was of course born a Catholic, raised a Catholic and died a Catholic. His interest in Buddhism was a discovery of different religious images for his fundamentally constant religious feelings. . . . It was just that, for a time, he was a self-taught student of Buddhism" (*Kerouac* 199). Once self-taught, he was soon eager to teach others. He dove into his studies of Buddhism with enthusiasm, encouraging his friends, especially the Cassadys and Ginsberg, to partake with him of "the one path." He even came to believe by 1955 that only poetry based on Buddhist principles would be without flaws (*Letters* 460). In a later interview Kerouac said, "My serious Buddhism, that of ancient India, has influenced that part in my writing that you might call religious, or fervent, or pious, almost as much as Catholicism has." When the interviewer asked him to identify the differences between Jesus and Buddha, Kerouac responded, "There is no differ- ence" (Berrigan 556–57).

When Kerouac discovered Buddhism, he had recently completed *The Subterraneans,* and as he told interviewer Al Aronowitz, "I went home and just sat in my room, hurting. I was suffering, you know, from the grief of losing a love."[1] The First Noble Truth of the Buddha especially intrigued Kerouac: Life is suffering. More generally, the ancient Indian term *duhkha* means more than suffering; it refers to the condition of people who do not have what they want or have what they do not want, who sorrow and grieve, or who are ill. Some Bud- dhist commentators use the word *anguish* as a translation, and Kerouac himself once stated the First Noble Truth thus: "All Life is Sorrowful" (*Good Blonde* 166). The First Noble Truth matched up with how Kerouac had felt throughout his life, par- ticularly regarding his professional career. He had written five books since the spring of 1951 without any publication. He had been thwarted in his main desire: professional recognition of his success as a writer. In the dedication to *Howl* Ginsberg identifies Kerouac as one of the "best minds" of his generation being destroyed by the mechanistic, unsympathetic American culture. In fact, Ginsberg called Kerouac the "new Buddha of American prose."

In 1954 Kerouac began writing Buddhist studies and trans- lating Buddhist sutras from the French. He kept a notebook that swelled eventually to hundreds of pages of Buddhist translations along with his ideas on their importance and meaning. He called this book *Some of the Dharma,* and it was finally published in 1997. This book is certainly not a concentrated study of Buddhism; it reveals, instead, Kerouac's own eccentric approach to Buddhism. He does include a smattering of scholarship—a Buddhist bibliography, for example, and some translations of ancient texts—but mostly the book consists of his apparently unadulterated speculations on the general notions of what Buddhism meant to him. The book might not be of use to a beginning student in Buddhism, yet it is intriguing because the reader can follow Kerouac's mental elaborations as he processes Buddhism through his thoroughly Christian value system. From the start Kerouac contrasts one savior with the other: "Buddha goes beyond Christ" (1). A surprising aspect of *Some of the Dharma* is its portrayal of Kerouac's ongoing battle between spiritual enlightenment and his desire to write. Throughout the book he recognizes that no words can convey truth properly; the Buddha's teaching is beyond words. Furthermore, he believes that his attempts to write merely serve to feed his ego unless he can write the Duluoz Legend so that every line provides enlightenment (278, 279).

Kerouac was impressed with the huge epochs of time, the *kalpas,* that lead cyclically to vast new ages. In the face of such colossal patterns, one's ego vanishes to insignificance. The editors of *Jack's Book* point out other parallels between the Buddhist universe and Kerouac's. For example, he found in "the notion of *dharma,* the same self-regulating principle of the universe that he had proposed himself in the closing pages of *Doctor Sax. Maya,* the illusory play of reality, matched the vision of his personal insignificance" (Gifford and Lee 186). Kerouac also identified with the Buddhist notion of compassion for all living things, a lesson his brother, Gerard, had taught him years before. Though his frenetic interest in Buddhism would wane later in his life, Buddhism affected nearly every subsequent book Kerouac would write, an influence foregrounded even in the titles of *The Dharma Bums* and *Satori in Paris.* Interested readers should refer to the biographies, letters, *Some of the Dharma,* James Jones's *A Map of* Mexico City Blues, and *Big Sky Mind: Buddhism and the Beat Generation* (see the bibliography) for more details of Kerouac's involvement with Buddhism and its effect on his art.

Thematically, one of Buddhism's more important influences on Kerouac was its insistence on abstinence. While he never quit drinking entirely—and recognized this as a weakness—he did swear himself to celibacy for most of a year. While he lusted for Mardou in his pre-Buddhist *The Subterraneans* and assumed that his male readers were similarly "crudely sexual" as well, in *Tristessa* Kerouac assumes the persona of a celibate penitent, mindful of his Buddha nature. Later he would boast that he had endured a year of celibacy because he saw lust as the cause of birth, which in turn brought about suffering and death (*The Dharma Bums* 29). Besides celibacy, Kerouac found the doctrine of impermanence to be important. He had always sensed the fleeting quality of life and reflected this in his writing, and now he began to see that even the apparent reality of the present moment was illusory. All the sensations of the physical world were merely an entrapment in samsara, the karmic wheel of death and rebirth.

Kerouac saw in the Buddhist concept of nirvana an escape from illusion and grasping, a return to the Eden he felt he had lost. Nirvana represented the completion of his life's seeking, for he moved first from the bliss of his mother's womb, then from the security of his father's house, and finally from the idealistic philosophical notions that might have sustained him in his youth. After a period of loss Kerouac believed he could regain the sense of bliss again through Buddhist meditation and awareness.

On a more communal, less personal level, Kerouac found in Buddhism an alternative to the cold war culture that surrounded him. Carole Tonkinson, editor of *Big Sky Mind,* explains that from the Buddhist point of view, "Cold War catchwords—us and them, ally and enemy—were rendered meaningless. . . . And Buddhism's advocation of a mendicant, homeless life also suggested the practical alternative to the rapidly accelerating cycle of work-produce-consume that was the engine driving fifties' culture."[2] Kerouac relied more on the personal aspects of Buddhism in *Tristessa, Visions of Gerard,* and *Desolation Angels,* and he developed the social, cultural ideas in *The Dharma Bums.*

Tristessa

When he arrived in Mexico City in the summer of 1955, he wrote his long poem *Mexico City Blues,* his first artistic attempt to convey his Buddhist-inspired visions. Immediately after finishing his poetic Buddhist exploration, he began *Tristessa,* a prose exploration of a related situation. He based the main character on Esperanza Villenueva, who served as a morphine connection for Kerouac's friend Bill Garver. In keeping with the mood of the book, he changed her name from Esperanza, which means "hope" in Spanish, to Tristessa, which means "sadness." Although the jacket notes of most editions say that Tristessa is a prostitute, it is difficult to find evidence in the text to support that claim.

Kerouac continues the Duluoz Legend in Mexico City from an entirely different perspective from the way he presented his affair with Mardou in *The Subterraneans*. Again, he positions himself as a narrator excluded from the central cast of those he observes and with whom he interacts. However, in *Tristessa* he focuses on the difficulties of maintaining compassion among a group of Mexican junkies who have little to offer anyone besides Tristessa's sexuality, which Duluoz denies himself. Instead, he comes to see that she possesses an innate sense of Buddhism without having ever read the works he himself has studied. There is a tragic consequence in her ability to cancel desire, though. As Kerouac transcribes her speech, "I weeling to haff jonk—morfina—and be no-seek any more" (28). Tristessa is saying that she will not be *sick* anymore, since for an addict a shot of morphine cures its own disease. Yet Kerouac implies that this drug is still a temporary form of nirvana, a release from desire (seeking) and thus from pain, however temporary. Tristessa also lives according to the Buddhist doctrine of karma: she understands that life is hard, and she says, "What I do, I *reap*" (28). Tristessa knows, too, the Buddhist precepts of impermanence. She tells Duluoz that since both she and he will die, they are "nothing" (76).

Buddhism blends with Catholicism in this book. Just as Kerouac saw the subterraneans as "Christlike," he sees Tristessa as the "Virgin Mary of Mexico" (13). Like Kerouac, Tristessa is a devout Catholic. She keeps a large icon in her room, but the Catholic imagery extends beyond a traditional representation of piety; Tristessa's companion, El Indio, prays devoutly before the icon when he goes out to buy drugs. They keep their Catholic attributions in Kerouac's descriptions just as the subterraneans remain Christlike as they smoke marijuana and inject heroin. In this tale, though, the characters take on both Buddhist and Catholic aspects. For example, Duluoz admits that he knows everything is all right, but still he wants "proof and the Buddhas and Virgin Marys are there to remind me" (19). Later he prays to "*ma Dame*" and accentuates the *Dame* "because of Damema the Mother of Buddhas" (38).

Very little happens in this story, for the core of Duluoz's experience here is observation and reflection, not action. When the narrative begins he is drunk; he takes a shot of morphine at his hosts' behest; and he observes the scene around him without interfering. A key scene occurs when Duluoz troops home at night through the rain. Viking Press adviser Malcolm Cowley once wrote to Kerouac that *Desolation Angels,* a later book, was formless and weakened by the impression that "Duluoz seems to be moving through his own reflections almost in a world of ghosts."[3] Kerouac responded that this was precisely his intention. These books did not satisfy Cowley's expectations for what a novel should be, while in fact the books are a different genre altogether—dramatized events from real life, heightened by artistic language, based on interior considerations of external circumstances.

In his earlier spontaneous prose stories Kerouac blends memory, reality, and dream to achieve the perception of events by the mind. In *Tristessa* he adds the element of unreality. As Kerouac writes in *Mexico City Blues,* "Dharma law / Say / All things is made / of the same thing / which is a nothing" (66). This apparent paradox is at the core of Buddhism. Nirvana comes when one sees the wholeness of the universe, yet even the notion that there is a "wholeness" is an illusion. There can be no "wholeness" as long as there is a separate perceiver to see it. Throughout *Tristessa* tears appear in the fabric of reality as Kerouac reveals the lack of substance one usually takes for granted. For example, as Duluoz observes Tristessa preparing her morphine shot, he inexplicably recalls a scene from his youth. In that scene he now realizes that his surroundings are not only impermanent but are beautiful *because* they are not lasting (23). This end of things is more than the dissolution of form Kerouac saw in *Doctor Sax* as the high school fence posts disappear, and more than the loss of the riverbanks in *Maggie Cassidy.* For now, Duluoz sees beauty in their cessation because they were never there to begin with. The things end because the perceiver realizes their impermanent nature and sees that they are simply manifestations of maya.

As Duluoz walks home through the rain, he observes a group of children who have just finished playing a baseball game. A player acknowledges a bad play he has made but adds, "Didn't I make it up with that *heet* in the seventh inning?" (55). Again, Kerouac uses the Mexican pronunciation to produce a pun, for *heet* means "hit" but also implies "heat," the totality of the player's involvement in the moment when he made his good play. One tenet of spontaneous prose is that the words stay as written. A jazz musician cannot retrieve a passage he has just played, and Kerouac will not retreat in his writing to undo what he has just done. Joyce Carol Oates notes that "to say that Kerouac's work is uneven is simply to say that it is Kerouac's work."[4] Still, Kerouac will frequently roar back with eloquent passages that, like the kid's hit, are the heat that make up for the miscues. Another level of meaning is possible here too. The idea of karma means that one is responsible for one's actions, and in some future existence one must atone for the actions of the present life. Tristessa, despite her addiction to drugs, believes that the Lord will reward the good she does. Duluoz knows that she will reap her reward, that she will receive blessing in nirvana (27). Duluoz, too, hopes to atone later for present actions. He arrives home Sunday morning, and though he falls asleep while other people are going to church, he avows to make up for it later. In fact, the next paragraph, ostensibly written after he sleeps, is a prayer—"Blessed Lord, though lovedest all sentient life"—that is a mixture of Buddhist and Catholic imagery.

Part 2 begins a year later, after Kerouac had lived the adventures that would become *The Dharma Bums* and *Desolation Angels.* Nonetheless, he nearly seamlessly stitched part 2 onto the end of part 1, manipulating the phrase that ended the first part to begin the second. Still, strong differences in mood reveal that much has changed in the year that has passed. For one thing, Duluoz now regrets his celibacy as a mistaken notion, for he now feels that their intimacy may have helped her (84). Since the previous summer, Duluoz has learned the vaguely Buddhist practice of *yabyum* (described in *The Dharma Bums*), where sex is a celebration of life and togetherness. For another thing, Tristessa's insistence that she is "seek" is obviously the case now, for she has been addicted to morphine all this time and has also begun taking "goof balls" (Seconal).

As in his other books, Kerouac includes the rhetorical decisions he must make about the writing process in the text of the book itself. Early in part 2 he states that since he does not remember all the details of the story except the final night, he will avoid the writer's traditional urge to "build up" (86). Kerouac wishes to avoid the trappings of telling a story in a predetermined form, a "literary" form, that would rob it of its essential interest, which for him is the emotional impact of events. Years later he told an interviewer that "FEELING is what I like in art, not CRAFTINESS and the hiding of feelings" (Berrigan 541). As he moves toward completion of this book, then, he consciously attempts to avoid relating a structured version of the events and instead offers a series of impressions. The color blue dominates the scenes as Bull Garver and Duluoz go downtown to El Indio's place to buy drugs. The day leads to Duluoz's own kind of blues, as he complains, that his poems and his money have been stolen, that Tristessa is sick; he had not imagined his pitiful fate (109). Not even his language can save the sense of despair; "O I wish I could write!—Only a beautiful poem could do it!" (112).

Finally, Tristessa's desire for morphine overrides any hope that she and Duluoz could be together. After he tells her he now wants to marry her, she reveals that her true love is morphine. Perhaps Garver and Tristessa will be together, though, for Garver says that one must be a junkie to understand a junkie (122). Duluoz takes a shot of morphine so that he can be temporarily more like them, and the prose of the book dissolves in wordplay and loose association. Life becomes a movie that shows God to people and people to God, and Duluoz's part is to chronicle the "long sad tales about people in the legend of [his] life" (126). *Tristessa* is not a fully developed exploration of its main character as *Visions of Cody* is, but Tristessa is not really at the core of this story. Instead the book explores Kerouac's relationship with Buddhism and the language he invents to reveal that relationship.

Visions of Gerard

One phrase in *Tristessa* was so important to Kerouac that he wrote it in capital letters and vowed to write it all over America: "BORN TO DIE." Impending death made no sense to Kerouac, for it seemed to negate or make insignificant all the labors and sufferings of life. Only a mystical, spiritual comprehension could counter the senselessness of the inevitable death of humans; death is not life thwarted, for death and birth naturally arise together, as wet implies dry, or as high implies low. Kerouac offers in *Tristessa* a message "that recompenses all that pain with soft reward of perfect silent love" (33). The apparent senselessness of death and the message that alleviates the suffering it causes are at the core of *Visions of Gerard.* A biographer of Beethoven once wrote, "Few men have the capacity fully to realize suffering as one of the great structural lines of human life." Stephen Batchelor, who cites this line in an article on Buddhism, goes on to say that "as with Great Dharma, Great Art begins with an unflinching acceptance of anguish as the primary truth of human experience. . . . All are united by the terrible beauty of anguish."[5]

For four years no other person was as close to Kerouac as his older brother, Gerard;[6] in fact, Duluoz identified so strongly with his older brother he claimed that he *was* Gerard (2). Without Gerard's saintly influence, Kerouac says—through the persona of his narrator, Duluoz—that he would not have become a writer. Kerouac also firmly believed that his brother was a saint. Warren French finds that "considered as a saint's life, *Visions of Gerard* is a remarkable achievement for a twentieth-century writer generally regarded as an instigator of a counterculture" (66). Gerard's life had other lasting effects, too, for Duluoz swears that their mother loved Gerard more than she loved him (72). Gerard was an inspiration, a tragic loss, and an unwilling combatant for their mother's affections.

In *The Town and the City* Kerouac writes of his parents' lives before he was born. He develops their characters and fills in their experiences; in short, he fictionalizes them, for he had no firsthand knowledge of their lives at the time covered in the early parts of the book. Kerouac wrote in a 1950 letter to Cassady that when he wrote those characters, he was "trying to stuff" his material but that he would not succumb to that ploy again. However, Kerouac wrote an entire novel about the brother who died when he himself, called Ti Jean by his family, was only four years old. He even tells Cassady that he barely knew Gerard and remembered little of their relationship. He goes on to relate one clear memory of Gerard (*Letters* 255). He also recalls that, just before Gerard died, Gerard slapped him in the face for disturbing his erector set project. He even admits in the text of the novel that his "memory is limited and mundane" (109). One wonders, then, how Kerouac could get the material to write this novel while he seems to remember clearly only two events. In part, he relied on stories his parents and relatives told him through the years. His long letter to Cassady contains most of the scenes that he would retell in the novel, and his source was family lore. Gerard apparently was a fixture in the family legend—his stories repeated "a thousand times"—before Kerouac wrote him into the Duluoz Legend. He relies also on his ability to romanticize the scenes that must have occurred and to invent scenes that probably did not occur but serve to balance the story. Finally, Kerouac wished to express the spiritual embodiment that Gerard was for him. If his lasting impression of Gerard was necessarily distorted by the fact that he had perceived as a four-year-old does, the distance between fact and impression is of little consequence. Kerouac portrays Gerard the way he saw him; after all, this is the Duluoz Legend, the saga of his own life blown to legendary status. Whether or not Gerard did or said the things attributed to him in this book is not as important as whether Kerouac believes he did. He later wrote in *Desolation Angels* that he may only remember a few of the things Gerard said to him as a child, but he knows that Gerard spoke of "a *reverence* for life, no, at least a reverence of the *idea* of life, which I translated as meaning that life itself is the Holy Ghost" (229). *Visions of Gerard* is the most "fictional" or "creative" book in the Duluoz Legend. As Kerouac concludes Gerard's tale in his letter to Cassady—his few memories and the stories that his family had relayed—he claims, "if you burned what I write you now with such joy I could never tell it again so truly; so of course, don't burn anything but save for me, for my honest books of later" (262).

In twelve nights in January 1956, writing by candlelight and under the influence of Benzedrine, Kerouac wrote the tale of his brother's last year. He wrote what he thought of as a variation of Shakespearean prose. He told Ann Charters that he had recently read *Henry V* and the Elizabethan diction had influenced his own style. Kerouac's manner in this book is quite different from that of his previous books—which were different from each other as well. Long sentences, quirky twists and associations, and word-play predominate as in the others, but this book contains a softer, more religious tone.

Kerouac begins the tale with a variation on the classic invocation to the muse: he imagines that Gerard would "bless my pencil as I undertake and draw breath to tell his pain-tale for the world that needs his soft and loving like" (3). The rhythm is basically iambic ("the world that needs his soft and loving like"), a Shakespearean characteristic. Kerouac also reveals his method of composition, as he writes with a pencil and structures his phrases and sentences according to his natural breath. The verb "undertake" puns on "undertaker," referring both to Gerard's imminent mortality and to the last scene, based on another pun, when the gravedigger "picks up his shovel and closes the book" (129). The puns tie the book together, as Kerouac uses the pencil temporarily to revive Gerard and the gravedigger uses his tool as an implement of closure.

Throughout the book the narrator jumps from his narration of his family's past to describe recent events. Besides being a typical Kerouac technique that reveals the writer at work, this temporal leap also distances the past, when Gerard lived, and the present days, when Gerard is lost. For example, young Ti Jean watches as Gerard befriends a hungry kid and asks his mother to feed his new friend. Duluoz adds that on a recent trip to Lowell he has seen the now-matured kid who has grown to six feet tall and weighs two-hundred pounds (5). The implication is that although Gerard is gone, his kindness still lives on in the form of a grown man who benefited from it. The most important connection between the past and the present is Kerouac's Buddhism, for of course there was no Buddhism in the Kerouac household when Gerard lived. Kerouac's Buddhism percolates throughout the story that had no Buddhist flavor for his family when they told and retold the events. Duluoz imagines Gerard watching the dissolution of summer clouds that, in their immateriality, reflect Taoist principles (2). The people of the town and even the solid redbrick smokestacks—and Gerard himself—will similarly dematerialize. Clouds work as symbols of the impermanence of reality since they seem solid, possessing color and shape, but no one can grasp them, and they disappear when observed for any length of time. Like Tristessa, Gerard has an intuitive knowledge of the fleeting nature of things. He proposes that reality is as transitory as the smoke from his father's pipe (25).

One night Gerard goes to the store to get aspirin for his mother, an act that typifies Gerard's kindness. Gerard travels through the cold night with which Frances confronted Peter in *The Town and the City* (42). Gerard avoids the spiritual implica-

tions of the terrible, cold night, though, by arriving at a fundamental Buddhist conception. Were it not for Gerard's presence as
a perceiver, he understands that there would be no cold, that the
feeling of cold is merely the sensation of his interaction with the
environment. Without that sensation, people would see the world
as heaven and know that there is no future salvation to await.

The book also features Christian—specifically Catholic—
imagery, from the parochial school Gerard attends to the church
itself and finally the funeral mass. Gerard is Christlike when he
angrily admonishes the cat who ate his mouse in a manner rem-
iniscent of Jesus chastising the moneychangers in the temple.
Gerard's Christlike qualities are coupled with Buddha-like qualities. In the biography of the Buddha, young Sakyamuni leaves
his royal father's walled-in house and discovers the suffering of
the poor and the old. In the cold night Gerard crosses paths with
the solitary old junk man, who is coming home with his burden-
some junk cart. The sight leaves Gerard shaken, and he wonders
why God put people out of heaven to be sick and cold.

The key scene in the book plays directly in the title: Gerard's vision of heaven. The nun is reciting a catechism, the oral
recitation and memorization of Catholic principles, taught in
question and answer. Because of his illness Gerard has not slept
well, and now he dozes in class. In his dream he recounts his
responsibility to take care of his little brother, Ti Jean. Then Gerard sees the Virgin Mary, a beautiful emanation of purity (52). In
this dream Gerard's suffering existence on earth is but a brief
morning when he wandered out of heaven. Ti Jean himself will
have this awareness at Gerard's funeral, when he cannot understand the grief the adults suffer. Ti Jean senses that Gerard's

death means his freedom from suffering, and in any case, life is "a dream already a long time ended and [my parents] don't know it and I try to tell them, they want to slap me in the kisser I'm so gleeful" (111). In the midst of this gloomy book of a child's illness and death, Kerouac yokes Buddhism and Catholicism and announces that Nirvana and Heaven reside in the present moment (110). As with other mystics throughout history, Gerard is frustrated at his inability to convey adequately the substance of his vision. He says on Christmas Eve, the last for which he will be alive, that he wishes eagerly to tell his family of his understanding of heaven—the visions of Gerard—but he fears these matters cannot be put effectively into words (59).

As in most of his earlier books, Kerouac pays close attention to seasons and their significance in the story. In one particular set piece Kerouac launches into a paean to spring. In keeping with his Buddhist knowledge, he immediately notes that spring, as generally recognized, is the time of rebirth. Now, however, he realizes that the rebirth only leads to more death. He manipulates syntax to bring the two significant terms into the closest possible contact: "Comes the cankerous rush of spring, when earth will fecundate and get soft and produce forms that are but to *die, multiply*" (74, emphasis mine). Readers arrive at the word "die" before the word "multiply," for no doubt exists as to the fate of living things. Kerouac uses the term "cankerous," which has an appropriate sound for the "rush of spring" yet contains also connotations associated with "canker"—an open or festering sore, a source of corruption—and comes from the Latin root "cancer." The hopeful song of spring is riddled with the inevitability of disease.

Almost as an escape from the pain of Gerard's sickness, Duluoz continues by detailing an evening with the father, Emil, based closely on Kerouac's own father. As Emil meets his friend, Manuel, in the warm airy night, Kerouac records the sounds that float through the open windows and attributes a human cause to every one. The cacophony creates a kind of human symphony, with the orchestra ranged around the neighborhood; the evening gathers up human utterances and activities in its swirling current and carries them along in an endless stream (81). In his wildest prose experiment, "Old Angel Midnight," (1959) Kerouac would return to another evening when he listened to the sounds of the universe coming in his window. For now, he is content to list the sounds without trying to imitate them—except for standard onomatopoeia.

As *Tristessa* did, *Visions of Gerard* ends with Kerouac describing the reality of life as if it were a movie directed by God (127). The movie conceit is Kerouac's representation of maya, which Kerouac employs in several other books as well. The child Ti Jean and the adult narrator Duluoz each feel compelled to tell people of the "*Here* and *Now*" of salvation, but each is frustrated in his attempts to make that message clear. They share a vision of heaven that might be impossible to pass on through the medium of language, whether oral or written. Nonetheless, Kerouac conveys his Buddhist-influenced perceptions on the long-ago events that shaped him as a person and as a writer.

CHAPTER NINE

Desolation Angels (1965) and *The Dharma Bums* (1958)

The summer after Kerouac finished *Visions of Gerard,* he spent two months as a fire lookout on Desolation Peak in the Cascade Mountains in western Washington state. His friend Gary Snyder, a poet and student of Buddhism (and the hero of *The Dharma Bums*), had encouraged Kerouac to take the job, one he himself had done in the past. Neal Cassady had set Kerouac up for a railroad brakeman's job, and Kerouac had learned more about Cassady's world firsthand as he expanded his own. Now he was poised to learn more about Snyder's. He had another goal too. By spending the summer in isolation atop a mountain, he hoped to achieve some kind of spiritual break-through: a satori, or sudden enlightenment. This would be another kind of quest, but instead of the constant motion and escape of the automobile, he would be absolutely stationary; instead of listening to jazz he would observe the silence of the stars above the mountain. Just as in *Visions of Cody,* Kerouac would face again the task of inventing and refining the proper language and style to embrace his subject. Along with *The Town and the City* and *Visions of Cody, Desolation Angels* is one of Kerouac's most ambitious projects, for once again he seeks to "explain everything to everybody."

As he had done with his experiences with women in *Maggie Cassidy, The Subterraneans,* and *Tristessa,* he would turn his solitary fire-lookout job into an opportunity for writing a

book. He kept a journal on the mountaintop from which he drew
to write the first section of book 1, "Desolation in Solitude." He
wrote the second part of book 1, "Desolation in the World,"
about his attempts to maintain the insights he had gained on the
mountain when he reentered the American culture. In 1961 he
wrote book 2, "Passing Through," although the events he records
there took place immediately after those of book 1. Book 2
focuses on Kerouac's travels to Mexico, New York, Tangiers
(Morocco—sometimes spelled "Tangier" or "Tanger"), France,
London, and back to America. Originally conceived as two
separate books, they combine to form the longest work he had
written since *The Town and the City*. Besides being written five
years apart, the two books of *Desolation Angels* were also written pre- and postfame. Book 1 was probably the last major
writing Kerouac did before the onslaught of fame hit him after
the publication of *On the Road* in September 1957. In fact,
after Kerouac produced *The Dharma Bums* in ten typing sessions in late 1957, he wrote no other substantial work until he
finished *Desolation Angels*.

Desolation Angels

Since *Doctor Sax,* in which Kerouac explores a fantasy of his
adolescence, he had taken greater liberties in exploring his
matured self as the central subject in his writing. *Maggie Cassidy, The Subterraneans, Tristessa,* and *Visions of Gerard* each
focus on a distinct character, even though the narrator views
them from his own particular perspective. In the beginning of
Desolation Angels, though, Kerouac (again his alter ego is Jack

Duluoz) is alone on a mountaintop. Duluoz had begun the trip with the confidence of a pilgrim or sojourner to a wise man's lair: he predicted that once in solitude, he would penetrate to the core of human existence and understand "God or Tathagata" (4). Instead, he finds only himself confronted by a vast, silent mountainscape. Weeks later he finds the answer he had come for by paying attention to that mountainscape that was affected neither by all the activities of people nor by the decay of time. Finally he understands that even that mountain will fall apart, that it is only "passing through" like he is. His satori, then, is the awareness that one must simply *be* and not try to understand all the mystery in the show of forms—that is, in the manifestations of the void— because ultimately nothing in the universe is really happening. He discovers his motto: "Shut up, live, travel, adventure, bless, and don't be sorry" (5). In his solitude, though, he frequently thinks of being elsewhere, so one may wonder whether his insight is less permanent and affirming than he believes it to be.

The story does not really begin until Duluoz finishes imparting his lessons in poetic prose, grappling with the inability of language to describe reality, and then returns to the cities of his Beat Generation friends. When he began book 2 after four years of literary infamy, social notoriety, and heavy drinking, he could only say that his insights and his freedom had become overshadowed by the ways of the modern world when he returned to it (220). In the first sentence of *Desolation Angels,* he evokes "those afternoons, those lazy afternoons, when I used to sit, or lie down, on Desolation Peak" until he found a profound sense of peace. As he prepares to rejoin civilization, Duluoz announces that he would carry with him the lessons he had learned on the mountain top and share his visions with his friends. He would find, though, that his friends, "involved in the strictures of time and life," had been absorbing lessons of their own (66). Kerouac puns with *Time* and *Life,* for those are the magazines that were about to belittle him and those friends as the new wave of literary rebels.

As literary fame looms, Duluoz feels more trapped. In the end, he loses the dynamism that animated him in his youth and sustained his writing prowess, and he resolves to remain at home with his mother in "peaceful sorrow" (366). Paradoxically, Duluoz becomes ensnared in the net of America that he himself helped tie. *Desolation Angels* is, more than any other Kerouac work, a book about America. Early on he refers to his "beloved America" (11), and he does not worry about the problems that afflict other countries because "America is as free as that wild wind, out there, still free, free as when there was no name to that border to call it Canada" (19). Kerouac relates the "free" America to the Canada of his forebears, and he also ties in his satori of personal spiritual freedom with the idea of American freedom. As he had done at the end of *Visions of Cody,* Kerouac again finds in Cody a metaphor for America, yet every year the laws and the authorities were reining in the fun (363). "Law Ridden America" is a bastardization of Kerouac's pure, original America and serves also in this book as a metaphor for the limits of one's spiritual freedom. Just as people could no longer go joyriding without inciting police suspicion, people too must be wary of the entrapments of their spiritual independence. Kerouac finds no lasting way to keep his spiritual attainment in modern America and thus yearns for the romanticized America he perceived in his childhood.

Kerouac summons up the character of America as it reveals itself in different seasons. The first cool breezes of autumn cause him to think of the World Series and of football games that would be broadcast coast-to-coast on the radio (32). When he comes down from the mountain he looks into the current baseball news and eats an ice cream cone, activities as typically American as one can imagine. Much later he will recover from an opium overdose in Morocco and wish for "Wheaties by a pine breeze kitchen window in America" (317). Yet either America—drawn largely from Kerouac's childhood impressions—is overly romanticized or else its character is changing. Kerouac values kindness and understanding, but neither American citizens nor its authorities share his usual acceptance—at least tolerance—of his friends' wild behavior. Instead of kindness, Kerouac complains, the world imposes order, and this imposition limits one's liberty (205). One of his off-the-mountain battles, then, is to sustain a balance between personal freedom and the limits that Law Ridden America places on its citizens. Instead of the America that is "as free as that wild wind," Kerouac fears a future industrial state that will burn out her resources and rob her of vitality (31). A more biting example of America's authoritarian rule is Jarry Wagner's (based on Gary Snyder) being blackballed from forest service work because of his vague communist connections. An old-time forest service worker warns that wayward statements now lead to FBI investigations (59).

The last image of book 1—the same image begins book 2—is of a busload of young men on their way to prison. Duluoz is on a bus to the freedom of Mexico where he can live cheaply and write without interruption (and smoke marijuana and enjoy prostitutes under the lax authority of the Mexican police system), while on the parallel road twenty young men are bound for incarceration. As book 2 begins, Duluoz hitchhikes toward Mexico; policemen with spotlights accost him. The physical presence of the police is metaphorical evidence of his fear of lost freedom in America. Kerouac concluded a short piece, "The Vanishing American Hobo," written some years earlier, with the warning that "the woods are full of wardens" (*Lonesome Traveler* 183). Gone is the wilderness he wrote of in *On the Road,* the frontier days of Ben Franklin, George Washington, Daniel Boone, and freedom-loving adventurers pushing westward (*On the Road* 105). To hear Kerouac tell it, America's founders were her first Dharma Bums, yet the unmistakable tone of school history lessons and the sheer simplicity of Kerouac's version of the settlers' lives reveal his keen joy for the way things might have been.

As usual in Kerouac's writing, the book is also about the art of written expression. Each of his books presents its own specific rhetorical challenge: the picaresque episodes of *On the Road* and the need to convey the energy of the times; the supernatural adolescent nostalgia of *Doctor Sax;* the hagiography of *Visions of Gerard.* In *Desolation Angels* Kerouac attempts yet another form, one that suits a wandering Zen Lunatic (or as he admits, "a Drunken Lunatic") amid the lures of society, including sex and alcohol (219). Traditionally, wandering Zen masters have no trade; they live off alms people offer them. Kerouac, though, must write, and he finds himself in the bind of writing the adventures as he lives them in the first book and from a distant perspective in the second. The difference is apparent; in the latter half he tries to justify the life he had lived, while in the first half he is closer to the action, more of a recorder.

Kerouac's essential romantic nature has loosed a mysterious "something" throughout most of his work, that dark and unnameable element that flits just out of sight. Now Kerouac begins to comprehend the patterns of those actions and to see those patterns as part of the great illusion of reality. Unable to apprehend directly the nature of reality in the awesome moun-tainscapes, Kerouac listens instead to the desolate fragments of human voices on his radio as the other solitary lookouts check in nightly to share staccato conversations. In the same way his memories provide him with clear, detailed images of his past that arrive unbidden (11). Kerouac initially does not confront the nature of the void; instead he populates it with imagination and memory. He recalls, for example, specific details of his child-hood fantasy baseball league. In that sense the isolation catalyzes thoughts and maybe even insights, but he does not achieve a state of blank-mindedness, one goal of meditation. If he had, his jour-nal might have been empty, a perfect Zen expression of the emptiness of forms. But Kerouac cannot *not* write; it is in his nature to do so. He puts his natural disposition as a writer into poetic form: "The candle burns / And when that's done / The wax lies in cold artistic piles / ———s about all I know" (71). His writing life is the burning; his books are what is left.

Duluoz's descriptions often lead to insight and often, too, to futility. In his best moments the insight and futility arise together. After describing the mountains and the inherent power behind them, he breaks off abruptly: "this bleary dream of existence is just a blear in its—I run out of words" (28). Language fails him, and he resorts to drawing triangles and abstract squiggles. The next several pages are simply abstract lists of words, strung along for their sound. One gets the impression that the author is murmuring to himself as a form of consolation. Yet Duluoz also implies that words are useless in the conveyance of truth. Gradually sense intrudes, order again begins to infiltrate the language, and Duluoz describes the moon, finally finding a way out of the sounds of nonsense.

Just as he had done in *Visions of Cody,* Kerouac follows the "nonsense" babbling section with some of the finest and most inspired writing in the book. Here his discovery of bear droppings one morning leads him to contemplate the void; yet now he succeeds in the writer's task of finding a suitable metaphor to convey its awesome power. The bear itself does not appear, for he is the "unseen monster" that stalks "somewhere in that Zen Mystery Fog." The great bear is at once terrifying and yet powerfully alluring and possesses the ineffable enigma that Kerouac seeks (56). In this passage Kerouac shows his ability to combine nature writing and spiritual exploration.

In the most insightful report Kerouac made from his experience, he tries to render himself invisible and instead be the vehicle for the universal essence: he envisions, paradoxically, that there is "nothing to say" (64). Kerouac has already pointed out the paradox that "nothing" is all there is, so "nothing" is what must be said. "Nothing" can be a positive capacity, as in Wallace Stevens's poem "The Snowman," where one is admonished to see nothing that is not present and "the nothing that is." When he finished writing the journal he was calling "Desolation Adventure," he concluded that he preferred narrative—storytelling—to nonlinear verbal exploration and believed that this kind of writing was not "suitable" for his capabilities. Kerouac's strength is in his ability to combine narrative events and his feelings on those events. On Desolation Peak nothing happened, and that "event" can be unsettling for a writer.

The rest of the novel is in fact a narrative, generally simple and direct. Duluoz passes through one adventure and then another, selected from Kerouac's own life, each recorded in detail. As Duluoz hitchhikes, motion, a new energy, enters the story. On the mountain readers encountered revery and meditation, but now Duluoz is "passing through," braced by the lessons from the mountain. Duluoz's task now becomes the "narrative rundowns of what I saw and how I saw" (220). The theme through these journeys is that change is painful (67). Growing old, death, loss of friendships, loss of spiritual reassurance—all these changes create confusion and pain. At one point Duluoz depicts this change by combining memories and present observations: he describes the excitement children felt as they played in old junkyards in Lowell, but now grown men recognize that the junkyard's message is one of inevitable decay (64).

Writing is one way of preserving the past unchanged, at least from the perspective of the writer. Kerouac possessed the ability, as attributed by poet Robert Creeley, "to translate immediate sensation into immediately actual language" and to record experience in writing with "no impedance" (Nicosia 521). Kerouac's spontaneous prose pulls life from the moment via life's own flow, out of that shifting, ungraspable moment—the "jewel center"—without contrivance or plotted technique. Kerouac's prose is an artifact, a frozen statement of both the moment of the event and of the moment of its composition. In *Desolation Angels* the conscious writer is aware too that writing does not last either, and he frequently questions its value. Still, the candle burns; the wax piles up. In spite of his realization that nothing lasts, Kerouac lives for the high moments, when he is with his friends and they are sharing joyful discussions of poetry, when they are, in fact, living life itself as a poem (134), and this is the flow that Kerouac has re-created on the pages. Kerouac gives his readers the passing days of his life after the mountaintop job and the influences of his friends and his times in America on his Buddhist beliefs. That his enthusiasm for Buddhism and his purity after the mountain will fade will be the most significant of the vicious changes.

The first of his friends Duluoz speaks to upon his return to San Francisco is poet Raphael Urso (based on poet Gregory Corso), and Duluoz insists that Raphael's poetry be spontaneous. He explains that the best poetry comes when one writes without stopping, without thinking to mask one's innermost feelings (128). Duluoz goes with his friends Urso, Irwin Garden (based on Allen Ginsberg), and others to the home of an art patron before a poetry reading. In the middle of dinner the Beat poets begin to shout non sequiturs that bounce off each other's ideas. After the dinner Duluoz is disinclined to attend the poetry reading. Although Duluoz would enjoy conversing with the poet—a spontaneous exchange—he does not wish to hear his formulated verse: "I'd rather hear Raphael's new bombs of words" (184). Duluoz listens to one line the poet recites ("The duodenal abyss that brings me to the margin of my consuming flesh") before heading out to a bar to meet young women and listen to jazz.

Despite Duluoz's attempts to avoid the literary world of polite salons, delicate readings, and the claptrap of the publishing business, he is unable to dodge his fate. On the one side, Irwin Garden implores Duluoz to enjoy the fame, money, and travel that accompany a writer's recognition (252), while on the other hand Duluoz recalls his now-deceased father's prediction that Irwin Garden and Hubbard (based on William Burroughs) would ruin his family's good name (286). The path down from the mountain leads to fame and notoriety, and Duluoz copes partially by drinking excessively. His new life, which he had hoped would be "a peaceful sorrow at home," combines with his furious city life at the expense of his writing.

The Dharma Bums

Sometime in the fall of 1957 Malcolm Cowley suggested that Kerouac write a sequel to *On the Road.* Kerouac complied and told Cowley, "I'm mighty proud to let you know that I have just finished a new novel, written like ON THE ROAD on a 100 foot roll of paper, single space, cup after cup of coffee, the last chapter infinitely more sublime than anything in ROAD and the whole thing quite different."[1] Kerouac was referring to *The Dharma Bums,* his book about Gary Snyder and "the rucksack revolution"; the events it describes occurred six years after the events at the end of *On the Road.* It is a "sequel" because the central characters from *On the Road* (those based on Jack Kerouac, Neal Cassady, and Allen Ginsberg) reappear along with Kerouac's new hero, Gary Snyder, named Japhy Ryder in this book. Biographically the book is a sequel because it recounts Kerouac's own adventures; the author maintains the first-person point of view, this time as Ray Smith, a name left over from an early, unfinished version of *On the Road*. Why Kerouac did not use the Duluoz name for himself here is unclear, but the only Duluoz book published so far was a Grove Press book, and he wrote this one specifically for Viking. The change in name could have had something to do with Viking's fears that characters in the book could be recognizable and might sue for libel. Kerouac assured Cowley that it was "a real American book and has an optimistic American ring of the woods in it." For the first time in his life Kerouac felt like a professional novelist rather than a neglected artist. *On the Road* was on the best-seller lists, and as he explained to Ginsberg, he felt like a good novelist and that *The Dharma Bums* was a better book than *On the Road*. He worried, though, that he might not stay sober enough to finish it.[2] Kerouac did not write *The Dharma Bums* while drunk; his reference to sobriety in this letter refers to his inability to cope with the pressures of fame and notoriety in the aftermath of *On the Road*'s publication, and specifically to his upcoming appearances at the Village Vanguard, a Greenwich Village nightclub, in December 1957.

The Dharma Bums, finished in ten marathon typing sessions, was accepted quickly at Viking. *On the Road* had sold well, and *The Dharma Bums* was just the sort of book Viking wanted from Kerouac. It contained no experimental prose, and the story unfolded in linear time with identifiable characters and set situations. The writing was exuberant enough that Viking could package the book as the continuing quest of Jack Kerouac, author of the previous successful book. Kerouac had at least five completed but unpublished novels that he would rather have seen in print—and more than sixty notebooks filled to the margins with his scrawled prose—when he put himself to the task of producing *The Dharma Bums.* Undeniably—and understandably—he was cashing in on his overdue renown. He was also under the influence of Malcolm Cowley, the father figure who had almost single-handedly brought Kerouac into print, first in excerpts and then with the complete *On the Road.* To write *The Dharma Bums* Kerouac listened to Cowley's advice and wrote a new book that was not in accord with the writing principles he had worked out through years of trial and error. Like *On the Road, The Dharma Bums* was written rapidly, yet in a conventional style. *The Dharma Bums* represents the kind of success Kerouac might have enjoyed had he not sacrificed commercial prosperity for artistic integrity. J. Donald Adams had used the occasion of the publication of *The Subterraneans* to criticize the Beat Generation in his "Speaking of Books" column in the *New York Times Book Review.* After reading some new material Kerouac had published in *Holiday* magazine that stylistically paralleled the prose of *The Dharma Bums,* Adams had a change of opinion: "I find it necessary to revise certain opinions expressed [in this column concerning Kerouac]. Offhand I would say that when Kerouac sets his mind to it he can describe the world of physical experience better than anyone since Hemingway. When he writes unaffectedly and unselfconsciously, but with control, he writes very well indeed."[3] Important, too, is the fact that Adams did not object (in his column, at least) to the miscegenation, the drugs, or the general immorality of the lifestyle represented in *The Subterraneans;* the prose style offended him.

Like *On the Road, The Dharma Bums* begins with the narrator noting that the good times are already over by the time of composition. In this work Smith recalls that since the time of the story, when he was devoted to his religious practices, he has "become a little hypocritical about [his] lip-service and a little tired and cynical." Instead of being "so much sadder and perceptive and blank," as are the central characters in *On the Road,* he is now "grown so old and neutral" (5). In another oblique reference to the earlier work, Smith considers himself at the beginning of the story to be a "Hero in Paradise" (5), a title that evokes the name Sal Paradise. Just as Paradise was inexperienced and listless at the beginning of *On the Road,* Smith relates that he had not yet met Japhy Ryder, so there is a strong sense of the adventures that are yet to be, of another pearl to be discovered.

One big difference between the books is Kerouac's incorporation of Buddhism. As in his other Buddhist works, Christianity combines with Buddhism to produce the distinctive Kerouac religious flavor. Here, for example, Smith shares a boxcar with a bum who reads Saint Teresa's prayer aloud every day. This figure is the first Dharma Bum encountered by Smith and sets Smith up for his meeting with "the number one Dharma Bum of them all" (9). Though Smith has been leading his version of a Buddhist life, he needs Ryder to show him how to cope in the modern world. Once he knows the tricks, he vows that he feels wholly revitalized (77). When Ryder outfits him with a new poncho, pack, and camping gear, Smith claims, "I felt like a new man" (107). However, he is not a new man; he is the same man made over. He still holds within himself his traditional notions of

Catholicism. Smith sees Ryder as a frontiersman, and thus an American hero, but he can never free himself from the trappings of his own memories of and devotion to Catholic imagery. He seeks his own particular blend of both Catholic and Buddhist dogmatic perspectives. Once he asks Ryder, "Isn't Heaven Buddha's nirvana?" Ryder tells him that he is limited by his own interpretation (114). A woman street preacher approaches Smith and tells him that she recognizes his sympathy for her message. Although Ryder does not like "all that Jesus stuff," Smith says confidently that he hears her message and understands it (114–15). At one point Smith prays to "O Buddha thy moonlight O Christ thy starling on the sea" (117). However, frustration confronts Smith in both sets of beliefs, for Smith ultimately finds that the truth is ineffable and resides beyond the dominant images of both Buddhism and Catholicism (137).

Alvah Goldbook (based on Allen Ginsberg) pronounces Ryder to be a "great new hero of American culture" because of his intelligence, his knowledge of poetry (specifically of Pound and Asian poets), his use of mind-altering drugs for visionary purposes, and his love of hiking and camping in the wilderness. Ryder is decidedly distinct from Moriarty, whose energies do not sustain him after the road adventures. Ryder is the healthy alternative; he scales mountains on foot instead of racing down highways in cars; his certainty of spiritual values comes from his study of centuries of Eastern philosophy; and his relationships with women are far more sharing and responsible than Moriarty's. Besides, Ryder is multifaceted, for while Goldbook admires his scholarship and his visionary outlook, Smith likes his often quiet ways and his sad dreamy moments. In Ryder,

Smith finds a fellow seeker who has gone farther along the path of Buddhist practice and who can therefore validate his own spiritual understandings. Like Moriarty, Ryder seems more authentic than the narrator, who again puts himself in the position of one who follows dutifully. Instead of escaping into the moment via jazz, dope, and drink, though, Ryder offers the opportunity to escape the spiritually stifling aspects of civilization by literally stepping out of it, into the wilderness where one can survive on cunning and woods lore. Ryder quickly isolates Smith's predicament, telling him that he would be happier if he could escape the snarls of modern urban life and enjoy communion with nature (69).

Smith's delight in his newfound self-sufficiency is soon undercut, though, by an acquaintance's senseless suicide. Rosie, one of Cody's girlfriends, is involved in the kind of paranoia of law enforcement that tugs at Smith only loosely. Even Smith's strong Buddhist convictions cannot save Rosie, for as usual he lacks the means to make clear to her the simplicity of the universe that is obvious to him. Meanwhile, Rosie tries to convince Smith that *she* possesses the real knowledge and that they are all in danger of imminent arrest. Rosie falls from the roof of a building in a bizarre parallel to the boxcar bum's prayer of Saint Teresa, where roses fall from heaven. Her suicide represents the result of the police state (real or imagined) that she felt threatened everyone's personal freedom.

Her suicide convinces Smith to leave the city, and all he has to do is hop another freight train with his Ryder-inspired grip. Without Ryder's reassuring presence, though, Rosie's paranoia is contagious for Smith, who has run-ins with authorities that question the sanity of a man who purposefully sleeps along rail-road tracks. He tells a truck driver where he learned his "funny things" (129) and the significance of self-reliance. He does not impress his traditional family in Rocky Mount, though, with his hitchhiking, rucksacking, or his devotion to Buddhism, and they represent mainstream America. He attempts to explain his thoughts to them—as he does to his readers all along—but they respond that he should adhere to Catholicism, as it is the family religion (144).

Smith is aptly named, for the narrator is, as in all Kerouac's books, a wordsmith. While living the adventures he would later dramatize in *The Dharma Bums,* Kerouac had a realization that he shared with Gary Snyder: "Nirvana *is* Ti Jean L'Ecrivain!" (*Letters* 556). He is also constantly reminded of the difficulty he faces in communicating. Ryder, himself a poet, understands the futility of trying to express his spiritual understanding through language. He tells Smith that he is not interested in hearing a chain of words, for he prefers the illumination brought on by physical activity (169). Cody's enlightenment depends on action for the sake of motion, but Ryder's action is always productive. Smith learns from Ryder that "Twasn't by words he was enlight-ened, but by that great healthy push off the porch" (173). Ryder's actions include chopping wood and hiking in the mountains. Smith's action is writing. Kerouac concludes the book by describing his trip to Desolation Peak. Here he receives his holy orders to write, just as he had in most of his other books, this time from an enigmatic deity who combines Catholicism and Buddhism: "the Hearer and the Answerer of prayer said to me 'You are empowered to remind people that they are utterly free'" (239). Just as in *Desolation Angels,* the word *free* implies both personal and spiritual freedom—freedom in soul and freedom in America. Dean Moriarty disappears into the confusion of his life in America. Ryder goes to a meditation monastery in Japan. Smith returns to the world and writes this book.

CHAPTER TEN

Big Sur (1962)

Kerouac's overdue literary success destroyed him. He was ill equipped for dealing with the strong responses that his work, especially *On the Road,* evoked from both fans and critics. One of the ironies of Kerouac's life is that he initially had sought the fame of a conventional novelist. Critical attacks that savaged both his work and his personal life, the sudden assault of celebrity status, heavy drinking, and the likelihood that he felt guilty about using his friends' lives in his work combined to drive Kerouac to a breakdown in the summer of 1960. *Big Sur,* the novel he wrote about this breakdown, is a remarkable accomplishment, for in this work Kerouac traces the decay—and recovery—of his own rational mind.

Kerouac was aware of the tremendous difference between himself and the image the public had of him after his work burst into print in 1957. In one scene in *Big Sur* he recounts an afternoon when he is alone with an enthusiastic young man who obviously wants to impress the famous writer. The King of the Beats is tired of being pressed upon by a younger generation who, in their notions of some kind of Beat idealism, wish to share their lives with their idol. Kerouac knows that he is a disappointment to these young fans who expect him to jump with excitement (109). In fact, Dean Moriarty does most of the jumping in *On the Road* while the more introspective Sal "shambles after." He goes on to say that notes on a book jacket (Grove's first paperback edition of *The Subterraneans*) mistakenly reported his age to be twenty-five when he was in fact nearing forty. More than nine difficult years had passed since Kerouac had slipped a scroll of paper into his typewriter and hammered out *On the Road*. *Big Sur* works as a companion piece to this earlier novel; it provides a poignant sequel much more deeply than *The Dharma Bums* did; and it develops a counterpoint to the *Road* story and underscores the message of disappointment with road life that readers often miss. Taken with *The Town and the City* as opposite poles of the Duluoz Legend, *Big Sur* depicts the pathetic and perhaps unavoidable fate of young Peter as he hitchhikes out of the first novel, disillusioned with his past, into the adventures of the second book, setting him on a course that promises joy and leads to defeat.

The story of *On the Road* takes place between Sal's marriages; he leaves his past domestic life at the beginning and settles to a new one at the end. In *Big Sur* Jack Duluoz leaves his mother's house for the first time since the publication of "Road," which had led to constant attention from an overly inquisitive public, including drunken visitors who steal his books (5). At the end of the novel he returns to his mother. As in other novels, especially *The Subterraneans,* Kerouac's narrator returns home periodically after binges and traveling adventures. In this book Duluoz experiences a devastating but temporary mental breakdown that reveals to him how little he can rely on Buddhism. At the conclusion of *Big Sur* Duluoz responds to his mother's question in earlier books: "Why can't you stick to the religion you were born with?" Put in perspective, his mental anguish brought on by problematic drinking is another kind of adventure—certainly a dangerous one—from which he returns to the security of his mother's house (and her religion too) to write about the experience.

As in Sal's first *On the Road* adventures, Duluoz heads from the East of his home to the West of adventure. This time, however, he rides a cushy passenger train that makes his hitchhiking days seem part of a distant past of hardship; yet fame, as this book will show, brings its own misfortune. Now he is a famous writer and spends his money on luxuries such as the cross-country train ride, enjoying coffee and sandwiches. Duluoz keeps his faith in westward travel. As a group of friends heads to Big Sur singing traditional American sing-along tunes, Duluoz recalls some of the spirit that enticed him to head west in the first place: their westward trip replicates the action of America's frontiersmen and settlers (176–77). Every adventure in *On the Road* ends in temporary despair, usually a gray morning of hangovers and stale cigarettes. Sal always heads out, though, toward the promise the next evening holds. *Big Sur* opens on such a morning-after scene, but the despair is not temporary. The drinking of celebration and joy has become, over the years, a serious alcohol addiction that Duluoz realizes is threatening his sanity and probably his life. Years earlier Kerouac had made numerous references to his drinking problem in *Some of the Dharma.* The Duluoz Legend itself matches the subpattern of its component books and, as Weinreich shows in *The Spontaneous Poetics of Jack Kerouac,* the key rhetorical device within those books: the traveling and returning, the getting high and then crashing low. Kerouac shows his awareness of the apparently inevitable cycle when he quotes Thomas à Kempis: "You go out in joy and in sadness you return" (43).

At first Duluoz seeks the peaceful isolation that had been partially beneficial for him in *Desolation Angels.* He goes to Lorry Monsanto's (based on Lawrence Ferlinghetti) cabin near the coastal resort of Big Sur. In a gesture that symbolizes contrasts, he retrieves his rucksack with its essential survival gear from the bottle-strewn skid row hotel room where he has crashed. He takes the bus and a cab to Big Sur, and he must walk the last several miles to the cabin through darkness. The troubling notion that "something's wrong" constantly besets Duluoz, while the high cliffside road and the night's impenetrable darkness scare him. Even his trusty lantern cannot breach the darkness. In the morning he sees another scene that symbolizes the past of the Duluoz Legend: some years ago a car had crashed through the rails a thousand feet above, and the twisted remains of the car yet rust, embedded in the sand (15).

Although Duluoz seems to recover from his alcohol sickness, he foreshadows the events that lie in store. He states the date—September third, a night of the full moon—when he will suffer a mental breakdown (16). More than most of his books do, and certainly as opposed to *Desolation Angels,* this book possesses a strong sense of structure and control. The task at hand presents a rhetorical dilemma for the writer, for he contends with the nearly impossible task of describing a mental and spiritual crisis—a breakdown in his orderly thinking—in a well-structured book. Kerouac unifies the book one way by consistently undercutting the simple joys he finds in his first days at Big Sur with comments that hint at the dark future. For example, he may enjoy the babbling, playful sounds of the stream as it flows to the sea, but he tells the reader that he would hear that same pleasant sound transformed into a raving babble that will terrify him (20). He constantly notes that so many things seem pleasant, but he always completes the sentence with phrases such as "at first." Monsanto has left some novels in the cabin, and appropriately Duluoz reads *Dr. Jekyll and Mr. Hyde,* for he displays in his own book dual sides of his nature.

After three weeks Duluoz feels well enough to travel back to the city. His first hitchhiking attempt in years also points up contrasts with the legend of *On the Road.* After hours without getting a ride and being ignored by thousands of cars, he tries to walk the fourteen miles to Monterey, but he develops painful blisters on his feet. Duluoz agonizes over the change in the American drivers and families on vacation who only sneer at him or ignore him out of fear that he may be a Hollywood-inspired murderer. In a pleasant turn of events, the driver who finally stops exhibits charity and drives Duluoz all the way into Monterey. Such ends America's most famous road-goer's last hitchhiking trip. Another event is a farewell too. Later in the novel, in a confusing and desultory scene, Duluoz sees Cody for the last time (179).

Duluoz notices other changes in America, such as the housing developments along Bayshore Drive. While Peter in *The Town and the City* feels once that he has known "everything," Duluoz now cannot keep up; he becomes overwhelmed with the details of his life and his culture, and he copes by "swigging Scotch from the bottle" (65). The romantic nostalgia he feels for his childhood, his tight relationship with his mother, his production of confessional, romanticized novels—all these seem out of place as America sends rockets into space and superhighways conduct travelers quickly and innocuously to their destinations. Unable to find comfort either at Big Sur, where the sea's voice commands him to find human company, or in the city, where people expect him to buy drinks and meals, he escapes by hitting the bottle. At the time of the events chronicled in *Big Sur,* Neal Cassady had been recently released from San Quentin for a marijuana possession conviction. Although he denied complicity and faulted instead Cassady's high profile in San Francisco's North Beach bars, Kerouac must have felt some guilt for the arrest since his *On the Road* had made Cassady notorious. Now Cassady, Cody Pomeroy in the *Big Sur,* has also changed. Although Cody is not bitter about his time in prison—in fact, Duluoz remarks that he seems "more friendly"—the two men do not have the opportunity or perhaps even the energy to launch into the kind of conversation they enjoyed in the past. Because of their fame, they have been "hemmed in and surrounded and outnumbered—The circle's closed in on the old heroes of the night" (68). Cody also regrets Duluoz's heavy drinking, sensing that the alcohol is another factor that creates distance between them. Duluoz soon misses the healthy freedom of the Big Sur cabin, for in the city he feels trapped. Before the next important section of the book, he gives a matter-of-fact description of the onset of delirium tremens (74), and in the sections that follow, the reader can discern Duluoz's passage through each stage. Kerouac also structures the book by pointing out three specific "signposts" that foreshadow his coming madness (40, 49, 66) and then amassing "all the premonitions together" (51).

After a series of drunken parties in the city, Duluoz returns to the Big Sur cabin, but this time he brings a gang, only to find that the noise and clamor of the group "desecrate" the purity of the wilderness (94). The late-night gabfests find a sarcastic natural parallel as Duluoz observes that a "sinister wind" blows that seems too big for the small canyon (103). Images of death abound, from a series of nightmares to a floating dead sea otter and the mouse that died after Duluoz left out a can of rodent poison. Kerouac infuses every description of events or scenes with a powerful undercurrent of turmoil and threatening portent.

When Duluoz returns to San Francisco, Cody sets him up with Willamine, his mistress, whom they call Billie. Although she bores Duluoz, the "sad music of her voice" attracts him (146), and he agrees to marry her after one night together. One of the strangest characters in any Kerouac book is Billie's four-year-old son, Elliot, who seems able to read Duluoz's mind. Perry, a young man who is Billie's friend, is also strangely unfathomable. He responds to Kerouac's conversation with a pastiche of corny beatnik talk ("Who cares, pops, we're all swinging in love and trying to go from day to day with self respect while all the squares are putting us down"), yet for his silliness Duluoz thinks that Perry is really a dangerous character who may kidnap one of the preteen girls in the neighborhood (158). Events make increasingly less sense to Duluoz, and he begins to suspect the motives of everyone around him. After 174 pages of buildup, Kerouac concludes the section with a chilling line: "And this is the way it begins."

Duluoz decides to escape again to Big Sur, and this trip sets up his night of madness. Duluoz's state of mind deludes him into all manners of paranoia, from his friends deliberately plotting to make him crazy, to the upstream neighbors he suspects of poisoning the creek water. Duluoz cannot hide in anonymity, as he had done during his *On the Road* days; his name is in the newspapers Monsanto left in the cabin, recent gossip columns have already reported his elopement with Billie, and he imagines that the vacation-goers at Big Sur see him as a decadent author who invades their wilderness retreat with parties of drinkers and prostitutes (184). He finds no solace in the city, he regrets instantly his decision to return to Big Sur, and the road between has none of its old romantic charm or power to spirit him into the moment.

Duluoz had realized early while writing this book that since explanations are difficult enough, he simply will opt for telling the truth (29). For the old hack who is now a best-selling author, he is constantly aware of the drawback of rhetoric; it forces distance between the event and the writing about the event. He complains, "*Eh vache,* I hate to write—All my tricks laid bare, even the realization that they're laid bare itself laid bare is a lotta bunk" (41). Ordinarily he finds solace in the construction of stories and the piles of pages that result just as he enjoys building the mill race in the Big Sur creek, piling one stone on another and filling in the gaps. As Duluoz's faith in books and writing continues to wane, he notes that for Cody, living life has always been more important than writing about it since "writing's just an afterthought or a scratch anyway at the surface" (141). On the other hand, Duluoz has often said that writing is the purpose for his existence, so now he faces the poignant dilemma of continuing to write, which has led in part to his dementia, or to stop writing, a decision that would render his life meaningless (167). Just as in *The Subterraneans,* Duluoz cites honesty and inclusion of details as essential qualities of his writing, for the story is valuable only if he reveals the minutiae (19). In his descending madness, though, Duluoz begins to see his earlier attempts at writing as finger exercises and that he had been dabbling at a serious business. He vexes himself for having been too casual and carefree in his approach to writing (181); now he faces mortality and sees the tremendous seriousness of life as if for the first time. He feels that while he had written the proper words when describing the sensations of life, he has never before plumbed the depths of life's emotions. In the worst of his mental breakdown, he realizes that even though he had spent his youth writing about serious topics such as death, his own words were only now affecting him with their gravity (213).

The crucial moment in *Big Sur* arrives when Duluoz realizes the consequences of what he has done in his writing. When Duluoz begins the week of living with Cody's mistress, Billie, he brings the social baggage of a famous drunken author. He is pained to think of Cody's reaction to the way he has made Cody's private life public (150). He could be speaking just as well of his use of Cody—and others—for a character in his books. Kerouac's biographers mention the fear he had of alienating his friends since he drew largely on their actions, even the most private and sometimes painful, to write his books. Nicosia quotes Kerouac telling Cassady and a few others whom he fictionalized: "You people are gonna hate me when you read [*On the Road*]" (554). Now one of America's famous authors comes to feel that his current depressed state and borderline dementia are results of his nonchalant use of his friends' turmoil for material in his work. He vows that if he recovers from his current mental state, he will stop writing and become a mill-worker, thus undoing the life decision he made in *Maggie Cassidy* (150). Kerouac wrote in *Book of Dreams* that he should have continued playing football in college so that people would see him as a normal guy. Instead he became a writer, "which is so dangerous to my sanity—so that I may have to stop soon" (*Book of Dreams* 50). In fact, the justification for writing *Big Sur* comes on the last page when Duluoz vows to forgive the people he has been with during his madness "and explain everything (as I'm doing now)" (216). The last sentence in the book sounds a note of completion and finality, since "there's no need to say another word."

During his bout of madness at Big Sur, the constant flow of language that Kerouac had credited in letters as being the ongoing Duluoz Legend streaming in his brain becomes a cascade of crazy jabber. Once Kerouac had written to Malcolm Cowley that the Duluoz Legend was "one great dream with a unified spontaneous language lulling out the report forever so that in my sleep-bed the uproar continues" (*Letters* 516). Now that report has become a terror. The once reassuring sound of the creek as water tumbled over rocks transforms into a ceaseless, pervasive babbling that seems to originate not from the creek but from within his head (201). Duluoz believes that the babble is a message to him, telling him to die. In the midst of his delusions he recalls his home and his mother who waits for him there, and he asks her to pray for him. In this instant he makes a break from the Buddhism that had sustained his previous several novels. At one time he would have tried to realize the illusory nature of his pain and his confusion, regarding it all as samsara. Now he is too involved in the manifestations of his troubled mind, and he calls upon a personal God for salvation and upon his dearest human connection to be an intercessor. Just as he had seen "signposts" that foretold the mental trouble with which he is completely engrossed, he now seeks a sign that his God is there for him. As he imagines angels and devils vying for control of the sky, he sees a vision of the cross (205). Just as his brother, Gerard, had, more than thirty years earlier, Duluoz experiences a vision of salvation, a prophetic revelation of heaven. Unlike Gerard's, though, Duluoz's vision is not simple and radiant. Devils darken his revelation. Duluoz regrets his Buddhist studies and meditations for he now sees his salvation to be a Catholic one. Nonetheless, his night of ordeals is not over. As a kind of visitation to purgatory, Duluoz experiences hallucinations of bats and vultures. Even within these waking nightmares, the writer's mind engages occasionally. For example, Duluoz is the main participant in the horrible drama; yet at times he becomes the "Observer of the story" (208).

In the morning Duluoz finally falls asleep for a short time and finds that "blessed relief" comes to him almost immediately (215). His torture has passed, becoming only a memory from which he will create another book. The paranoia that possessed him disappears with neither a trace nor an explanation. Duluoz is as puzzled as Doctor Sax was when "the universe disposed of its own evil." Almost as a teaser to his subsequent work, Duluoz allows Buddhist images to filter like a mirage across his strong image of the cross, as he notes that he feels "Simple golden eternity blessing all," a softened blend of Buddhist and Catholic phrases. Readers may wonder whether Kerouac heightened the drama of his night in Big Sur, since the awful nightmares pass so quickly. Yet he himself admits that he does not understand the suddenness of its passing. Again he has been in the backseat of his own experience, the "Observer of the story," much as Sal Paradise is in *On the Road*. Kerouac takes himself to the edge of experience, whether that experience is sexuality, drugs, fast cars, bop jazz, religious and spiritual epiphanies, or madness, and he records the sensations that he feels. He cannot always explain what he sees there. In a sense, he is an American foreign correspondent, if one refers to the unknown interior of human consciousness as "foreign" territory. In *Big Sur* Kerouac probes deeper and more dangerous depths than in previous works, yet his role is essentially the same.

CHAPTER ELEVEN

Later Work

In spite of Kerouac's resurgence in popularity in the last twenty-five years, certain of his books yet linger in the ranks of ignored work. Not everything the man wrote finds legions of avid readers. Biographers may have plumbed two late novels, *Satori in Paris* (1966) and *Vanity of Duluoz* (1968), for their revelations of details of his life, but Kerouac neither established nor solidified his reputation with the publication of these books. They are plodding, often monotonous accounts of portions of his life, and they do not engage the reader with either the adventurousness of his earlier books or the vivified language that made much of his earlier work successful. Another late book, *Pic* (1971), is an amalgam of early writing and the writing Kerouac did late in his life in an attempt to complete the book. *Pic* has never attracted a large following, and critics seem unsure how to take Kerouac's attempt at re-creating dialect.

Pic is probably Kerouac's most curious book; it is unlike anything else he ever wrote. Tim Hunt reports in *Kerouac's Crooked Road* that, surprisingly, *Pic* represents a stage in the development of *On the Road*. According to Hunt, the first two drafts of the road novel are unpublished; *Pic* is the third draft, while *On the Road* and *Visions of Cody* are the fourth and fifth. While Kerouac lived at his sister's (Caroline) house in Rocky Mount, North Carolina, in the late 1940s and early 1950s he must have heard black boys talking and telling stories and been inspired to relate a tale from their perspective. The story Pic narrates consists largely of Kerouac's own travel adventures and his appreciation for jazz. Nicosia explains that the book as published (posthumously) in 1971 combines various early pieces of writing that Kerouac had saved throughout his writing career: "the central plot and characters came from the story he had written in 1951 about a North Carolina black boy named Pictorial Review Jackson [to which he added] the story of the Prophet on Times Square, first drafted in 1941 for the Young Prometheans' study group, a chapter about a fudge factory deleted from *The Town and the City,* and the full story of the Ghost of the Susquehanna, much of which had been cut from *On the Road*" (695). Kerouac patched *Pic* together in an attempt to make some money late in his career when he needed the income.

There is an important reason that Kerouac began *Pic,* though. After he finished *The Town and the City,* he was dissatisfied with his voice in the novel. He wrote to Cassady in 1950 that a major problem facing young writers is the selection of a voice for the narrator, and the chief criterion should be that the voice be authentic. Kerouac announced that he was going to write seven or eight books, each featuring an ethnically distinct first-person narrator (*Letters* 233). Although this mission to write books in different dialects is a product of Kerouac's bravado rather than of his serious consideration, he did in fact use various voices in his books, though nowhere so thoroughly as in *Pic.* Naturally, his characters usually had diction appropriate for their respective milieus, but he was seeking a narrative voice too. As this letter to Cassady reveals, Kerouac was in the process of deciding whether his books would feature the first-person narrator; *The Town and the City* had not, and his first versions of the road book were not in the first person either. One of the breakthroughs that came with his speed-typing stint for the scroll of *On the Road* was his decision to drop his attempts to tell his story through a fictional narrator and to assume a narrator closer to his own voice. *Pic* has a clear place in the development of Kerouac's writing. Kerouac first told his story, in its thematic essence if not in episodic detail, through the mouth of a young black boy before he retold the story via a narrator much more like himself. In fact, the parts of *Pic* that he wrote in 1950 represent Kerouac's first use of first-person narrator that has been published. All of his subsequent books feature first-person narrators.

Pic begins with the illness of the grandfather who has cus-tody of Pic, whose nickname derives from Pictorial Review Jackson, a slanted reference to Kerouac's own boyhood nick-name, "Memory Babe." Pic is an orphan, as is Sal Paradise in *On the Road.* In addition, Sal's story begins when he leaves home and the security of home life he had known with his wife. Pic repeatedly mentions how happy he has been in his grandfa-ther's house, so his relocation during his grandfather's hospi-talization represents a fall from bliss. Just as Dean Moriarty had arrived in New York to take Sal from his desultory existence, Pic's older brother, Slim, who had been unheard of for years, comes to take Pic away to a new life in the city. The novel is Pic's first-person account that he prepares ostensibly to let his grandfather know what happened to him after the grandfather was taken to the hospital. Despite numerous direct references to "Grandpa," there is no resolution or communication between the two. When the brothers finally arrive in California and meet

Slim's wife, the narrative is over with the grandfather apparently forgotten.

Although the story ends with ludicrous abruptness, most of the scenes within are well set up. For example, Pic hears hints about his family and its mysterious past before he learns the real history from his older brother, Slim. Also, before his brother arrives to take him to New York City, a cousin hints of the excitement and the lights that blare like a beacon when he shows Pic the "town" nearby and suggests what adults do there on "Satty night" (15). Pic, in his own way, manages to summon up a sense of urban excitement the way Kerouac's other narrators do: "ever'where I turn my ear I hear au-tos, and folkses talkin, and all kind of noises and music, I tell you, it was the noise of ever'body *doin somethin* at the same time all over with they hands and feet and voices, jess as plain" (40). Later Pic wakes up on the bus just as he and his brother enter New York, and his description of the lights of the city that glow in the purple sunset is Kerouac's twentieth-century urban response to Huck Finn's description of the sunrise on the Mississippi River (52–53). That is, Kerouac attempts to use Pic's natural diction as a vehicle to convey the subtly shifting lights and increasing activities as the bus enters the city in the same way that Twain used Huck's simple but flexible style and vocabulary to portray a poetic moment.

Pic's brother, Slim, is a black version of Dean Moriarty. He is city-smart and wily, both energetic and able to live by his wits. Like Dean, Slim has spent some time in jail and has become an outcast in his own family. His biggest connection with Dean is his ability to unfurl his ideas in a jazzy way, for

he not only plays a soulful jazz saxophone, but he also understands the importance of rapping: "I got a million ideas and
can shore pour them out of that horn, and I ain't doin so bad
pourin them without the horn" (62). Slim gets a gig playing in
a jazz combo, and his wife, Sheila, takes Pic along to hear the
music. Pic's description of the warm-up session matches Sal's
description of the jazz he and Dean listen to. These scenes may
have been Kerouac's own warm-ups for the writing he would
do in *On the Road* when he describes the jazz joints and his
and Dean's experiences in them. For example, this passage is
from *Pic:*

> [Slim] was holdin, and pushin that horn in front of him
> like it was his *life* he was rasslin with, and jess as solemn
> about it, and unhappy. And ever' now and then he make
> it laugh too, and ever'body laughed along with it. Oh, he
> talked and talked with that thing and told his story all
> over again, to me, to Sheila and ever'body. . . . One time
> he let out a big horselaugh with his horn, and hung on to
> it when ever'body yelled to hear more. (78)

In *On the Road* Kerouac sets up a nearly identical scene:

> [the tenorman] just hauled back and stamped his foot and
> blew down a hoarse, baughing blast, and drew breath,
> and raised the horn and blew high, wide, and screaming
> in the air. . . . laughed in his horn a long quivering crazy
> laugh, and everybody else laughed and they rocked and
> rocked. . . . (197–98)

On occasion Kerouac betrays his consistency in Pic's integrity as a genuine character. Once he has Pic—who has only recently uttered the ridiculous line "I never seed such many flies in all my born days" (11)—refer to Grandpa Jelkey as "serpentine" (12), a word more likely to be uttered by Zagg Duluoz than an uneducated boy. Later Pic compares Slim's sound on the saxophone to "a big New York City boat way out in the river at night," even though Pic has only been in the city for one day (75). In addition to those slips, though, one has difficulty believing that Pic's dialect is ever entirely genuine, for although Kerouac had a fine ear for speech—and his friends noted his success in capturing Mardou's voice in *The Subterraneans*—his knowledge of rural family life in North Carolina could only have been minimal. It would be easy, perhaps, to analyze Pic's speech and isolate linguistic inconsistencies, but one still must note Kerouac's ambition in attempting to animate and sympathize with a narrator so distinctly different from himself in the first place.

Satori in Paris is a slight but frequently humorous book that details Kerouac's 1965 ten-day trip to France. He was drunk nearly the entire time and failed to achieve his purported goal of researching his family heritage. He spent his money and his energy in bars and on prostitutes, yet he claims that he found, as he declares at the beginning of the book, "an illumination of some kind" (7)—a satori. As he rationalized during the composition of the story, his purpose is to demonstrate that every trip is a life-journey that modifies one's perspective (43). Although Kerouac insists that he achieved a sudden illumination, readers must look between the lines to find any evidence of the nature of that transfiguration.

Kerouac, who used his own name in this book so that he could report details of his genealogical study, found a different kind of family heritage, and maybe this discovery is the basis for his satori. Instead of discovering the distinct lineage of his particular family, he refers frequently to the relationship that all people share in the human family. In this way *Satori in Paris* represents a renewed attempt to convey the ideal of the brotherhood of man that had persisted in much of Kerouac's early work. Kerouac's drunken approach on his tour repels as many people in France as it attracts, and the book, for its garrulous gush of prose, can be said to have the same effect.

Kerouac announces, as he had in earlier books, a definition of literature that becomes the rationale for this work: literature is simply "the tale that's told for companionship and to teach something religious, of religious reverence, about real life, in this real world which literature should (and here does) reflect" (10). To energize the prose, Kerouac tells the tale in first-person, present tense and quickly shifts from scene to scene, often with dizzying abruptness. Having established the rationale, Kerouac comments on his method too, even as he lampoons his detractors. He imagines he can read the thoughts of a new young writer who regards Kerouac as an outmoded writer who has not kept up with the most recent literary trends. Kerouac responds by singing "Jimmy Lunceford's old tune: 'It aint watcha do / It's the way atcha do it!'" (54). Kerouac values style over substance.

On this trip Kerouac reverts to the image he has been developing of himself and his heritage throughout the development of the Duluoz Legend. Multileveled and often complex in his various guises in different works in the Legend, Kerouac portrays himself in France as a good American boy who is in trouble (69). Far from effecting the demeanor of a famous writer, he also sees himself as "some nut with a raincoat and hat" (71). In addition, he maintains the distance from Buddhism that had begun in *Big Sur:* "I am not a Buddhist, I'm a Catholic revisiting the ancestral land that fought for Catholicism" (69). Kerouac recalls dozens of conversations he shares in French with different people in different circumstances. His return to America reimmerses him in the world of the English language, and he marvels at the miracle of language: "what an amazing Tower of Babel this world is" (47). Kerouac expresses joy that language has the power to unite people and provide a vehicle for mutual understanding (47). Ultimately, *Satori in Paris* recounts a Kerouac adventure in a loose, conversational style that points, on occasion, to the deep affinity for humankind that Kerouac had always shared in his books. The book ends, though, like Kerouac's trip itself: foreshortened, with its meaning unclear.

One could claim that *Vanity of Duluoz,* like *Pic,* is also written in dialect—the dialect of a world-weary writer who "speaks" the words to his wife. Kerouac once told Ann Charters that he had written *On the Road* for his second wife to tell her of his recent road adventures. The same holds true for *Vanity of Duluoz,* a story which he tells to his third wife. This time the narrator addresses his wife directly as he reaches to the more distant past to recover his glory days on the football field, his time at sea in the merchant marine, and his introduction to the New York City characters who would change his life. Like some other Kerouac books, this one describes a series of events that are casually rather than causally related, but this book is not unified by any

tension from within or without. When Sal Paradise promises in
On the Road that "the adventures to come are too fantastic not to
tell" or that "the pearl" will be handed him, there is both the
sense that he means it and that readers' expectations will be ful-
filled. In *Vanity of Duluoz* the narrator announces that what he
has to tell about the United States Navy "will knock your head
off" (149), yet nothing of the sort happens. Still, the book represents Kerouac's late attempt to infuse his prose with another stylistic innovation, something that was lacking in the rather flat
Satori in Paris.

In his last book Kerouac revisits the period of his life he had
drawn on to write *The Town and the City; Vanity of Duluoz* also
begins in 1935 and ends in 1946. Both books end just after the
father's death. In fact, Kerouac briefly describes the composition
of *The Town and the City* at the end of *Vanity of Duluoz* as an
attempt to write "a huge novel explaining everything to everybody, to try to keep my father alive . . . and make a 'go' of it"
(266–67). Kerouac began writing *The Town and the City* soon
after the events that he describes in that book. But a darker element persists in *Vanity of Duluoz.* In 1967, aware that he was
writing near the end of his career—in fact, *Vanity of Duluoz*
would be his last book—Kerouac knew that his attempt at
"explaining everything" would be a vain effort. The title reflects
this double meaning of an attempt made in vain and the sheer
vanity involved in the challenge. Just as disillusioning was the
fact that his father had died despite his efforts to save him. In this
book Kerouac questions the significance of a life dedicated to
writing. Proceeding with full confidence in *Visions of Cody,* Kerouac had entertained no doubts of his mission to "redeem life

from darkness." But in reality, doubting his life's mission was nothing new to him. In 1954 Kerouac had written that his accumulated writings were but a "mass of nonsense" and that finally his Duluoz Legend amounted to "ripples on an endless sea" (*Some of the Dharma,* 221 and 278). In addition, the years of heavy drinking and critical attacks had blunted the enthusiasm the younger writer had possessed. By 1967 Kerouac's passions for Buddhism and Catholicism had waned. And yet *Vanity of Duluoz* can be seen as Kerouac's late, brave attempt to reinvigorate his prose and to summon a sense of grace in the relaxed, conversational language of a story that has as its main purpose the deflation of the narrator's earlier seriousness. Kerouac goes back to his origins as a writer and to the events that informed his first book to wrap up his career with a book that serves the Kerouac opus as a solid bookend opposite *The Town and the City.*

Kerouac notes in *Some of the Dharma* that in 1954 he understood the ultimate vanity of the Duluoz Legend, yet he never avoided the responsibility of writing as his human duty. Self-revelation had always been a major concern in his writing, and he predicted that "like Rembrandt in front of the mirror, I shall treat 'myself' like in third person and discuss my own vanity—nothing will be concealed in the end" (*Some of the Dharma* 278). The mirror represents both vanity and self-discovery. Self-discovery is a kind of vanity too. Nicosia notes that when Kerouac sat down to type *Vanity of Duluoz,* he positioned a mirror in front of himself. As previously noted, Kerouac sometimes looked up from his typing sessions to comment on the scene immediately before him—a radio, or the view from his window. In this case, raising his eyes from his typewriter could only return him to his subject, for in this book Kerouac seeks to justify his present circumstances. By recounting his past events, Duluoz (who also refers to himself occasionally as Kerouac) hopes to explain his "particular form of anguish" in which he now finds himself (9).

He will do more in this book, though; he will reconsider his approach to writing prose. He announces on the first page that he will not use the dash on which he had relied in his earlier spontaneous prose stories. The book is subtitled *An Adventurous Education,* a concept the narrator associates with allowing students to learn in their own ways, just as he skipped school frequently to read books in the Lowell Public Library and to study old movies in the Rialto Theater. "In these cases," the narrator insists, "the mind knows what it's doing better than the guile, because the mind flows, the guile dams up" (41). While Kerouac will not rely in this book on "deep form" or vertical pileup of details—characteristics of his finest spontaneous prose—he will allow himself the freedom to relate the events of his story casually, as his memory dictates to his hand. In *Vanity of Duluoz* the narrator portrays the mood not of the book's setting but of his own immediate frame of mind. He reveals his awareness of the difference between his present and earlier selves as he blends the two in the process of writing. When Claude (based on Lucien Carr) advises Duluoz of his defense before a judge, Kerouac writes, "'I know, you jape' . . . and 'you jape' I only just added now, in those days I just said 'I know'" (230). By drawing on the distinction between the past self—the serious writer—and the current self—the jaded writer—Kerouac reveals the vanity of the earlier self.

As in other books, Kerouac laments the loss of an idyllic America. Personally, he notes that he has become "eviscerated of 1930's innocent ambition" (16). From a broader perspective, he regrets that "people have changed so much" from the 1930s (9). Ironically, the author of *On the Road* wonders if the prominence of the automobile has reduced the joy and anonymity people once found in walking briskly to their destinations. In *Maggie Cassidy,* which is set in the 1930s, Kerouac recalls fondly the time when people walked from place to place in the open air, not confined behind the glass and metal of automobiles. He laments this change, as it represents a loss of neighborhood familiarity (112). As in *Desolation Angels,* it is the "vicious *change*" that causes anguish. So in its first pages *Vanity of Duluoz* hearkens back to the earlier, simpler times when young Duluoz played sandlot football. Duluoz establishes that simple life, then follows it through the complexity of college-level football, World War II, and the "low, evil decadence" of his life after the war.

A helpful way to gauge Kerouac's style in this book is to compare excerpts from *Vanity of Duluoz* that describe the same biographical scenes he drew on in *The Town and the City.* For example, one of the more memorable scenes in *The Town and the City* is Kerouac's romanticized re-creation of his high school football success in the big Thanksgiving Day game when Lowell High School beat its rivals from Lawrence. The game scene covers thirteen pages in *The Town and the City,* some four thousand words. Kerouac establishes the importance of the game with references to newspaper stories, radio coverage, and fans' speculation (74). In *Vanity of Duluoz* Kerouac re-creates the same scene in little more than one page, with approximately five hundred words. There is no buildup; the players are simply kids with whom he went to school, and the scene takes place with none of the earlier heroic representation. In this account Kerouac downplays the importance of his touchdown since his team was already winning the game. Kerouac mocks the players who feel that the day has epic status—"now the 'heroes' were ready and started without me" (22). He plays in the second half and scores his touchdown, an event that is followed simply by "pandemonium and et cetera" (23). Kerouac easily strips off his "New England nebulous style" that had characterized his earlier work. Instead of rendering the scene with hyperbole and exaggerated effects, he downplays both the significance of the game and his role in it, since he now senses the vanity in such portrayal: "you kill yourself to get to the grave before you even die, and the name of the grave is 'success,' the name of that grave is hullaballoo boomboom horseshit" (23).

There are many situations in the earlier book that are represented in the later book, and careful readers will find more distinctions of style and portrayal between the two. One more instance is worthy of mention, though. After his freshman year at Columbia, Duluoz stares up at the stars one night and then launches into an extended fantasy in which he leads his football team to the Rose Bowl and stars in the game; he passes his chemistry course with an A, runs a world-record mile, becomes the next Joe DiMaggio of baseball, achieves Faustian knowledge, writes prizewinning Broadway plays, becomes heavyweight boxing champion, and so on. He realizes even at his young age, however, that all his ambitions "came out fairly ordinary" (87). His human aspirations were not important in "space between human breathings and the 'sigh of the happy stars'" (87). In

The Town and the City Mickey Martin has the same starry musings (120), but he—like twenty-four-year-old Kerouac at the time he wrote the first book—is too young to consider the vanity of his longings for greatness and fame. Mickey dreamed of greatness: "There was never anything else that could hold his dreamy attention: all was the fulfillment of himself, the future, greatness, a heroic struggle and overcoming all obstacles" (120). Kerouac wrote *Vanity of Duluoz* to replace the earlier book's "nebulous" optimism, to erase its hyperbolic prose, and to reorient his own outlook on the world that had been tempered by age, experience, alcohol, and the ravages of the success he had once dreamed would be his. Duluoz's view of the universe is comprehensive and complex, "a maniacal Mandala circle all mosaic and dense with millions of cruel things and beautiful scenes" that resolves itself as a basic pattern of "Mother Nature giving you birth and eating you back" (262–63). The glories of life in between—on the football field, in war, in literary success—are merely flashes of vanity.

Introduction

1. Ann Charters, Edward Halsey Foster, Warren French, Gerald Nicosia, and Regina Weinreich all deal with the issue of Kerouac's construction of a legend. See the bibliography.

2. Charters, *Kerouac,* 357–58. Subsequent references are given parenthetically in the text.

3. For more detailed information regarding Jack Kerouac's professional dealings with editors, agents, and publishers, see Matt Theado, "Packaging Kerouac: Jack Kerouac and the Profession of Authorship," Ph.D. diss., University of South Carolina, 1994.

4. Weinreich, *The Spontaneous Poetics of Jack Kerouac,* 13. Subsequent references are given parenthetically in the text.

5. French, *Jack Kerouac,* xiii. Subsequent references are given parenthetically in the text.

6. Foster, *Understanding the Beats,* 65. Subsequent references are given parenthetically in the text.

7. Jones, *A Map of* Mexico City Blues, 5. Subsequent references will be given parenthetically in the text.

Chapter One: Biography and Background

1. Clark, *Jack Kerouac,* 3. Subsequent references will be given parenthetically in the text.

2. Nicosia, *Memory Babe,* 50. Subsequent references will be made parenthetically in the text.

3. Jarvis, *Visions of Kerouac,* 46. Subsequent references will be given parenthetically in the text.

4. Gifford Barry, and Lee, Lawrence, eds., *Jack's Book: An Oral Biography of Jack Kerouac,* 34–35. Subsequent references will be given parenthetically in the test.

5. Unpublished letter from Carolyn Cassady to author, 26 December 1998.

6. Holmes, "This Is the Beat Generation," 22.

7. *On the Road,* Penguin Classics Edition, New York: Penguin, 1991; xviii.

8. White, *Safe in Heaven Dead,* 34.

9. Ibid, 37.

10. Berrigan, "The Art of Fiction," 570. Subsequent references will be given parenthetically.

11. White, *Safe in Heaven Dead,* 40.

Chapter Two: Kerouac's Technique

1. Unpublished letter from Kerouac to Robert Giroux, 15 January 1962. Butler Library Rare Books and Manuscripts Room at Columbia University.

Chapter Three: *The Town and the City*

1. See Kerouac's unpublished *On the Road* work journal, Harry Ransom Humanities Center, University of Texas at Austin.

2. Tallman, "Kerouac's Sound," 519.

3. Kerouac revisited the same subject in one of his last books, *Vanity of Duluoz,* but his approach was totally different. See chapter 11.

Chapter Four: *On the Road*

1. Charters, *Bibliography,* 19. Subsequent references will be given parenthetically in the text.

2. Holmes, *Nothing More to Declare,* 79.

3. As already mentioned, Regina Weinreich deals with this issue in *The Spontaneous Poetics of Jack Kerouac,* 11 and 12.

4. Kerouac used his mother, Gabrielle, as the model for Sal's aunt.

5. When this selection appeared in *The Paris Review* before the Viking publication of *On the Road,* the sentence read "They thought I was a Mexican, of course; and I am."

6. A good, comprehensive etymology of the term *beat* appears in Steve Watson's *The Birth of the Beat Generation.* See bibliography.

Chapter Seven: *Maggie Cassidy* and *The Subterraneans*

1. Kerouac comes the closest to understanding his lover in *The Subterraneans,* but his descriptive comments on Mardou's experiences seem to be largely a product of his own fancy.

2. Kerouac's affair with Alene Lee occurred in New York City's Greenwich Village. He changed the setting to San Francisco before publication to avoid potential libel.

3. For firsthand insight, readers should consult Carolyn Cassady's own account in *Off the Road: My Years With Cassady, Kerouac, and Ginsberg.* See the bibliography.

4. The subject of Kerouac's possible racism is dealt with in detail in Ellis Amburn's biography, *Subterranean Kerouac.* Carolyn Cassady, however, claims that Kerouac's apparently racist and anti-Semitic outbursts were "superficial or transitory, gleaned from conditioning by his parents and others. It seems to me that by his easy acceptance of

both men and women of different races, his admiration for blacks, Mexicans, Indians, etc., he deserves a totally opposite judgment. Above all, he was tender hearted and compassionate" (letter to author, 12/26/98).

5. Unpublished letter from Jack Kerouac to Donald Allen, 19 March 1957. Mandeville Department of Special Collections, USC San Diego.

6. Letter from Kerouac to Neal Cassady, 23 July 1951.

Chapter Eight: *Tristessa, Visions of Gerard,* and **Buddhism**

1. Cited in Fields, "Buddhism Beat and Square," 75.

2. Tonkinson, "Buddhism and the Beat Generation," 60.

3. Unpublished letter from Malcolm Cowley to Jack Kerouac, 24 February 1957. Newberry Library, University of Chicago.

4. Oates, "Down the Road," 98.

5. Batchelor, "A Democracy of the Imagination," 71.

6. One should bear in mind that "Gerard" is pronounced differently in French than in English.

Chapter Nine: *Desolation Angels* and *The Dharma Bums*

1. Letter from Jack Kerouac to Malcolm Cowley, 9 December 1957, Newberry Library, University of Chicago.

2. Letter from Jack Kerouac to Allen Ginsberg, 30 November 1957, Butler Library, Columbia University.

3. Adams, "Speaking of Books," 2.

BIBLIOGRAPHY

Works by Jack Kerouac

Listed in order of publication: first American and first British editions

The Town and the City. New York: Harcourt, Brace, 1950; London: Eyre and Spottiswoode, 1951.

On the Road. New York: Viking, 1957; London: Deutsch, 1958.

The Subterraneans. New York: Grove, 1958; London: Deutsch, 1960.

The Dharma Bums. New York: Viking, 1958; London: Deutsch, 1959.

Doctor Sax: Faust Part Three. New York: Grove, 1959; London: Deutsch, 1977.

Maggie Cassidy. New York: Avon, 1959; London: Panther, 1960.

Mexico City Blues. New York: Grove, 1959.

The Scripture of the Golden Eternity. New York: Totem/Corinth, 1960; London: Centaur, 1960.

Tristessa. New York: Avon, 1960; London: World, 1963.

Lonesome Traveler. New York: McGraw-Hill, 1960; London: Deutsch, 1963.

Book of Dreams. San Francisco: City Lights, 1961.

Pull My Daisy. New York: Grove, 1961; London: Evergreen, 1961.

Big Sur. New York: Farrar, Straus and Cudahy, 1962; London: Deutsch, 1963.

Visions of Gerard. New York: Farrar, Straus, 1963; London: Deutsch, 1964.

Desolation Angels. New York: Coward-McCann, 1965; London: Deutsch, 1966.

Satori in Paris. New York: Grove, 1966; London: Deutsch, 1967.

Vanity of Duluoz: An Adventurous Education, 1935–1946. New York: Coward-McCann, 1968; London: Deutsch, 1969.

Scattered Poems. Ed. Ann Charters. San Francisco: City Lights, 1971.

Pic. New York: Grove, 1971; London: Deutsch, 1973.

BIBLIOGRAPHY

Visions of Cody. New York: McGraw-Hill, 1972; London: Deutsch, 1973.

Trip Trap: Haiku Along the Road from San Francisco to New York. Bolinas, Calif.: Grey Fox, 1973.

Heaven & Other Poems. Ed. Donald Allen. San Francisco: Grey Fox, 1977.

Good Blonde and Others. Ed. Donald Allen. San Francisco: Grey Fox, 1994. Includes "First Word" in "'First Word' Columns" from *Escapade;* "Are Writers Made or Born?" (77–79); "Belief & Technique for Modern Prose" (72–73); "The Rumbling, Rambling Blues" (40–44); "The Essentials of Spontaneous Prose" (69–71).

Book of Blues. New York: Penguin, 1995.

The Portable Jack Kerouac. Ed. Ann Charters. New York: Viking, 1995.

Selected Letters: 1940–1956. Ed. Ann Charters. New York: Viking, 1995.

Some of the Dharma. New York: Viking Penguin, 1997.

Selected Letters: 1957–1969. Ed. Ann Charters. New York: Viking, 1999.

Atop an Underwood: Early Stories and Other Writings. Ed. Paul Marion. New York: Viking, 1999.

Periodical Contributions

"Jazz of the Beat Generation." *New World Writing* (April 1955): 7–16.

"The Mexican Girl." *Paris Review* 11 (Winter 1955): 9–32.

"A Billowy Trip in the World." *New Directions* 16 (5 July 1957): 93–105.

"Essentials of Spontaneous Prose." *Black Mountain Review* 7 (Autumn 1957): 226–28.

Old Angel Midnight. Big Table I (Spring 1959): 7–42. Reprinted in book form, ed. Donald Allen. San Francisco: Gray Fox Press (1993).

BIBLIOGRAPHY

Wake Up. Tricycle (Summer 1993–Spring 1995). Kerouac's version of the life of the Buddha. Although originally slated to appear in *Some of the Dharma,* the *Tricycle* serialization remains its only appearance.

Interviews

Aronowitz, Alfred. "The Beat Generation." *New York Post,* 10 March 1959, pp. 4, 64.

Berrigan, Ted. "The Art of Fiction XLI: Jack Kerouac." In *On the Road: Text and Criticism,* edited by Scott Donaldson, 538–72. New York: Viking, 1979.

White, Michael, ed. *Safe in Heaven Dead.* New York: Hanuman Books, 1990.

Collections of Kerouac's Papers

Letters from Kerouac to Allen Ginsberg and from Kerouac to Lucien Carr are on deposit in the Butler Library Rare Books and Manuscripts Room at Columbia University.

Kerouac's "*On the Road* work journal"; the Knopf file concerning the submission of *On the Road;* letters from Kerouac to Carolyn Cassady, from Allen Ginsberg to Kerouac, and from Neal Cassady to Kerouac are in the Humanities Research Center at the University of Texas at Austin.

Letters from William Burroughs to Kerouac and from Kerouac to Robert Giroux are in the Berg Collection at the New York Public Library.

Correspondence between Malcolm Cowley and Kerouac is in the Newberry Library at the University of Chicago.

Correspondence between Donald Allen and Kerouac is in the Mandeville Department of Special Collections at the University of California, San Diego.

Works about Kerouac

Listed in alphabetical order by author.

Bibliographies

Anstee, Rod. *Jack Kerouac: The Bootleg Era.* Sudbury, Mass.: Water Row Press, 1994. Describes all known bootleg and pirated editions of Kerouac's work in the English language, 1969–1993.

Charters, Ann. *A Bibliography of Works by Jack Kerouac, 1939–1975.* New York: Phoenix Book Shop, 1975.

Milewski, Robert. *Jack Kerouac: An Annotated Bibliography of Secondary Sources, 1944–1979.* Metuchen, N.J., and London: Scarecrow, 1981.

Biographies

Amburn, Ellis. *Subterranean Kerouac: The Hidden Life of Jack Kerouac.* New York: St. Martins, 1998. A controversial study of racism and homosexuality in regard to Kerouac's life.

Cassady, Carolyn. *Off the Road: My Years With Cassady, Kerouac, and Ginsberg.* New York: Morrow, 1990. A firsthand, intimate account of Kerouac by Neal Cassady's wife.

Charters, Ann. *Kerouac.* San Francisco: Straight Arrow, 1972. The first biography of Kerouac by this groundbreaking scholar.

Clark, Tom. *Jack Kerouac.* San Diego: Harcourt Brace Jovanovitch, 1984. A concise and useful introduction to Kerouac's life and works.

Gifford, Barry, and Lawrence Lee (eds.). *Jack's Book: An Oral Biography of Jack Kerouac.* New York: St. Martin's, 1978. A compilation of dozens of interviews by people who knew Kerouac. Their comments are arranged to follow the course of his life.

Jarvis, Charles. *Visions of Kerouac.* Lowell, Mass.: Ithaca Press, 1974. A Lowell college professor recounts his interactions with Kerouac in their hometown.

Johnson, Joyce. *Minor Characters.* Boston: Houghton Mifflin, 1983. A well-written, emotional account of her relationship with Kerouac and the role women played during the height of the Beat Generation.

McNally, Dennis. *Desolate Angel: Jack Kerouac, the Beat Generation, and America.* New York: McGraw-Hill, 1978. Kerouac's life and work against the historical and social backdrop of his times.

Miles, Barry. *Jack Kerouac, King of the Beats: A Portrait.* New York: Holt, 1998. Miles discusses Kerouac's life largely in terms of his influence on society, particularly the "sixties lifestyle."

Nicosia, Gerald. *Memory Babe: A Critical Biography of Jack Kerouac.* New York: Grove, 1983. The most detailed biography yet written of Kerouac. It relies on hundreds of interviews and exhaustive research. Kerouac's biography should be updated now that more material has become available; historian Douglas Brinkley is currently working on a new, authorized biography.

Turner, Steve. *Jack Kerouac: Angelheaded Hipster.* New York: Viking, 1996. A short work grounded in biographical facts. Filled with photographs.

Articles

Adams, J. Donald. "Speaking of Books." *New York Times Book Review,* 18 May 1958, p. 2.

Batchelor, Stephen. "A Democracy of the Imagination." *Tricycle* (Winter 1994): 70–75.

Charters, Ann. "Jack Kerouac." In *Dictionary of Literary Biography,* Vol. 2: *American Novelists after World War II.* Detroit: Gale Research, 1972.

BIBLIOGRAPHY

————, ed. adviser. "Jack Kerouac." In *Dictionary of Literary Biography Documentary Series,* Vol. 3. Detroit: Gale Research, 1983.

Dardess, George. "Jack Kerouac." In *Dictionary of Literary Biography,* Vol. 16: *The Beats: Literary Bohemians in Postwar America.* Detroit: Gale Research, 1983.

Fields, Rick. "Buddhism Beat and Square." *Tricycle* (Fall 1995): 75–82.

Gussow, Adam. "Bohemia Revisited: Malcolm Cowley, Jack Kerouac, and *On the Road.*" *Georgia Review* 38 (Summer 1984): 291–311.

Holmes, John Clellon. *Nothing More to Declare.* New York: Dutton, 1967.

————. "This Is the Beat Generation." In *Kerouac and Friends,* edited by Fred McDarrah. New York: Morrow, 1985.

Oates, Joyce Carol. "Down the Road." *New Yorker* (27 May 1995): 95–98.

Tallman, Warren. "Kerouac's Sound." *Tamarack Review* 11 (Spring 1959): 58–74. Reprinted in *On the Road: Text and Criticism,* edited by Scott Donaldson, 513–30. New York: Viking, 1979.

Theado, Matt. "The Jack Kerouac Revival." In *Dictionary of Literary Biography Yearbook 1995,* 272–80. Detroit: Gale Research, 1996.

Tonkinson, Carole. "Buddhism and the Beat Generation." *Tricycle* (Fall 1995): 58–60.

Books

Donaldson, Scott, ed. *On the Road: Text and Criticism.* New York: Viking, 1979. In addition to the complete novel, contains hard-to-find articles and essays.

Feied, Frederick. *No Pie in the Sky: The Hobo as American Cultural Hero in the Works of Jack London, John Dos Passos, and Jack Kerouac.* New York: Citadel, 1964.

BIBLIOGRAPHY

Foster, Edward Halsey. *Understanding the Beats*. Columbia: University of South Carolina Press, 1992. A solid overview of the principal works of Kerouac, Ginsberg, Corso, and Burroughs.

French, Warren. *Jack Kerouac: Novelist of the Beat Generation*. Boston: Twayne, 1986. A useful study that divides Kerouac's personality between Peter and Francis, two brothers from *The Town and the City*. Kerouac's work is seen as a battle for control by each personality.

Hipkiss, Robert. *Jack Kerouac: Prophet of a New Romanticism*. Lawrence: Regents Press of Kansas, 1976. Cites Kerouac's significance in the development of American literature beyond the influence of the Moderns.

Hunt, Tim. *Kerouac's Crooked Road: Development of a Fiction*. Hamden, Conn.: Archon, 1984. An essential study of Kerouac's growth as a writer. Traces his progress from early drafts of *On the Road* through *Visions of Cody,* which Hunt claims is Kerouac's definitive version of his Road book.

Jones, James. *A Map of* Mexico City Blues: *Jack Kerouac as Poet*. Carbondale: Southern Illinois University Press, 1992. The first fully developed analysis of Kerouac's poetry, focusing on the long poem he wrote in Mexico in 1955.

McDarrah, Fred. *Kerouac and Friends*. New York: Morrow, 1985. Photographs, essays, reprints of feature articles.

Parkinson, Thomas. *A Casebook on the Beat*. New York: Thomas Crowell, 1961. An early study containing many mistakes, owing to the lack of access to primary source material Parkinson faced, but a fascinating analysis of the contemporary take on the Beat Generation.

Tonkinson, Carole. *Big Sky Mind: Buddhism and the Beat Generation*. New York: Riverhead Books, 1995. Tonkinson and her contributors trace the origins of American Buddhism, especially in its connection with the Beat Generation.

BIBLIOGRAPHY

Tytell, John. *Naked Angels: The Lives and Literature of the Beat Generation.* New York: McGraw-Hill, 1976. A serious literary analysis of the ways the principal Beat writers' lives influenced their artistic development.

Watson, Steve. *The Birth of the Beat Generation: Visionaries, Rebels, and Hipsters, 1944–1960.* New York: Pantheon Books, 1995. A readable overview of the origin of the Beats. Many fine photographs, useful maps, and charts of relationships.

Watts, Alan. *The Way of Zen.* New York: Vintage Books, 1957. Noted scholar of Eastern Philosophy, Watts helped introduce Buddhist precepts to the West in clear, readable books such as this one.

Weinreich, Regina. *The Spontaneous Poetics of Jack Kerouac: A Study of the Fiction.* Carbondale: Southern Illinois University Press, 1987. An essential study of Kerouac's technique that may be difficult for general students.

Journals and Periodicals Dedicated to Kerouac and the Beats

Listed in order of origin.

Moody Street Irregulars: A Jack Kerouac Newsletter. Begun in 1978 by Joy Walsh, this journal features contributions by Kerouac friends and scholars.

The Kerouac Connection. Originally published in Scotland beginning in 1984, this journal was taken over by Mitchell Smith in the United States in the 1990s.

The Dharma Beat. Edited by Attila Gyenis and begun in 1993, this journal is a forum for sharing various viewpoints concerning Kerouac and the Beats.

JUN 0 9 2000